Easy
Beading

Fast. Fashionable. Fun.

Vol. 3

The best projects from the third year of *BeadStyle* magazine

KALMBACH
BOOKS

Visit our Web site at
kalmbachbooks.com
Secure online ordering available

Publisher's Cataloging-In-Publication Data
(Prepared by The Donohue Group, Inc.)

Easy beading. Vol. 3 : fast, fashionable, fun : the best projects from
the third year of BeadStyle magazine.

    p., : col. ill. ; cm.

    All projects have appeared previously in BeadStyle magazine.
    Includes index.
    ISBN: 978-0-87116-241-0

1. Beadwork--Handbooks, manuals, etc. 2. Beads--Handbooks,
manuals, etc. 3. Jewelry making--Handbooks, manuals, etc.
I. Title: BeadStyle Magazine.

TT860 .E27 2007
745.594/2

Contents

On the cover
Page 172
Style set in stone

47

Glass and ceramic

79

Pearls and shells

97

148

178

Mixed materials

Crystals

144

Look for great shortcuts on these pages:
55, 87, 133, 175, 213

Introduction

Welcome to the third volume of *Easy Beading*. I have to say that this is my favorite so far, probably because I started at *BeadStyle* as its third year began. While I have an enormous appreciation for my predecessors' efforts, I tend to look at the projects created after I started with a greater affection.

For me, it's like a high school yearbook. All the projects have their own personalities. They elicit different feelings and memories. And since this is a graduating class of nearly 100, I know everyone will find projects they'll want to make their own.

This year's book includes four projects from "Beads of change," a department that has been a big favorite with the staff and our readers. The beads used in these

■ A BEADS OF CHANGE PROJECT

projects are made in communities around the world that rely on their sales to support the local economy. Each one is very different and beautiful in its own way. I encourage you to look at "Working glass heroes" (p. 30), "Bold beauty" (p. 47), "Small & beautiful" (p. 50), and "Keeping tradition alive" (p. 162).

Also new to this volume are icons that show you, at a glance, whether a necklace project is choker length, opera length, or somewhere in between. Look for these icons at the start of each project.

As in previous volumes, we've organized the third volume of *Easy Beading* by materials used: Glass and ceramic, Pearls and shells, Metal and chain, Gemstones, Crystals, and Mixed materials.

I know everyone has their own preferences – I am a fool for crystals – but I encourage you to check out every project. You can change materials and colors to suit your own tastes or the tastes of the lucky people for whom you may be making gifts.

There are projects for the beginner as well as the more-experienced beader. There are projects you can make in an hour or two and some you can tackle in 15 minutes. Get some Post-its ready and start marking your favorites.

I hope you have as much fun with them as we did.
Warmest regards,

Cathy

Cathryn Jakicic
Editor, *BeadStyle* magazine

Beader's glossary
findings, spacers, and connectors

French hook
ear wires

post earring
finding

hoop earring

lever-back
earring finding

earring
threader

magnetic
clasp

S-hook
clasp

lobster claw
clasp

toggle
clasp

two-strand
toggle clasp

box clasp

slide clasp

hook-and-eye
clasps

pinch crimp
end

crimp ends

coil end

connector
(crimp for cord)

tube-shaped and
round crimp beads

crimp
covers

bullion
wire

bead tips

jump rings and
soldered jump rings

split ring

spacers

bead caps

filigree
stamping

multistrand
spacer bars

double-curved
tube

single-curved
tube

three-to-one and two-
to-one connectors

bail

cone

ring
form

tools, stringing materials, and chain

crimping pliers

chainnose pliers

roundnose pliers

bentnose pliers

split-ring pliers

diagonal wire cutters

heavy-duty wire cutters

ring mandrel

twisted wire beading needle

tapestry needle

decorative head pin, head pin, eye pin

sterling silver wire

memory wire

colored craft wire

leather cord

suede cord

waxed linen

beading thread/cord

flexible beading wire

curb chain

rolo chain

long-and-short chain

figaro chain

cable chain

beads

Beads are available in a huge variety of materials, sizes, and shapes. Here's a guide to some of the most common that you'll find used throughout this book.

 dichroic glass

 glass nugget

 foil-lined bead

 lampworked bead

 glass flowers

 glass leaves

 teardrop

 fringe drops

 seed beads

 triangle

 cube

 Czech fire-polished

 bicone crystal

 cube crystal

 oval crystal

 crystal drop

 crystal briolette

 cone crystal

 round crystal

 saucer-shaped crystal

 top-drilled saucer (with jump ring)

 rhinestone rondelle

 rhinestone squaredelle

 rhinestone bridge component

 liquid silver

beads

gemstone
lentil

gemstone
rondelle

faceted button
or rondelle

round
gemstone

oval
gemstone

gemstone
rectangle

gemstone
tube

gemstone
drop

gemstone
nugget

donut

bone

horn

resin
nugget

chips

heishi

round
pearls

teardrop
pearl

potato
pearl

button
pearl

stick
pearl

petal
pearls

keshi
pearls

rice
pearls

coin
pearls

Basics

A step-by-step reference to key jewelry-making techniques used in bead-stringing projects.

plain loop

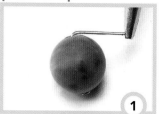

1 Trim the wire or head pin ⅜ in. (1cm) above the top bead. Make a right angle bend close to the bead.

2 Grab the wire's tip with round-nose pliers. The tip of the wire should be flush with the pliers. Roll the wire to form a half circle. Release the wire.

3 Reposition the pliers in the loop and continue rolling.

4 The finished loop should form a centered circle above the bead.

wrapped loop

1 Make sure you have at least 1¼ in. (3.2cm) of wire above the bead. With the tip of your chainnose pliers, grasp the wire directly above the bead. Bend the wire (above the pliers) into a right angle.

2 Using roundnose pliers, position the jaws in the bend as shown.

3 Bring the wire over the top jaw of the roundnose pliers.

4 Reposition the pliers' lower jaw snugly into the loop. Curve the wire downward around the bottom of the roundnose pliers. This is the first half of a wrapped loop.

5 Position the chainnose pliers' jaws across the loop.

6 Wrap the wire around the wire stem, covering the stem between the loop and the top bead. Trim the excess wire and press the cut end close to the wraps with chainnose pliers.

opening and closing loops or jump rings

1 Hold the loop or jump ring with two pairs of chainnose pliers or chainnose and roundnose pliers, as shown.

2 To open the loop or jump ring, bring one pair of pliers toward you and push the other pair away. Reverse the steps to close the open loop or jump ring.

split ring

To open a split ring, slide the hooked tip of split-ring pliers between the two overlapping wires.

surgeon's knot

Cross the right end over the left end and go through the loop. Go through again. Pull the ends to tighten. Cross the left end over the right end and go through once. Pull the ends to tighten.

overhand knot

Make a loop and pass the working end through it. Pull the ends to tighten the knot.

lark's head knot

Fold a cord in half and lay it behind a ring, loop, etc. with the fold pointing down. Bring the ends through the ring from back to front, then through the fold and tighten.

making wraps above a top-drilled bead

1 Center a top-drilled bead on a 3-in. (7.6cm) piece of wire. Bend each wire upward to form a squared-off U shape.

2 Cross the wires into an "X" above the bead.

3 Using chainnose pliers, make a small bend in each wire so the ends form a right angle.

4 Wrap the horizontal wire around the vertical wire as in a wrapped loop. Trim the excess wrapping wire.

folded crimp end

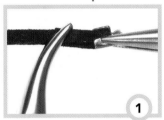

1 Glue one end of the cord and place it in a crimp end. Use chainnose pliers to fold one side of the crimp end over the cord.

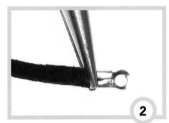

2 Repeat on the second side and squeeze gently. Test to be sure the crimp end is secure.

flattened crimp

1 Hold the crimp using the tip of your chainnose pliers. Squeeze the pliers firmly to flatten the crimp. Tug the wire to make sure the crimp has a solid grip. If the wire slides, repeat the steps with a new crimp.

2 Test that the flattened crimp is secure.

folded crimp

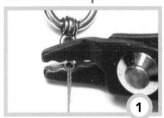

1 Position the crimp bead in the notch closest to the crimping pliers' handle.

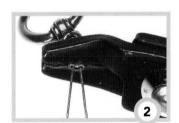

2 Separate the wires and firmly squeeze the crimp.

3 Move the crimp into the notch at the pliers' tip and hold the crimp as shown. Squeeze the crimp bead, folding it in half at the indentation.

4 Test that the folded crimp is secure.

Beads are sized using the metric system. This guide shows actual size in millimeters, a count of beads per inch, and a comparison to inches.

bead sizes	3mm	4mm	5mm	6mm	8mm	10mm	12mm
beads/in.	8.25	6.25	5.0	4.25	3.25	2.5	2.0

1   2   3   4   5   6   7

Glass and

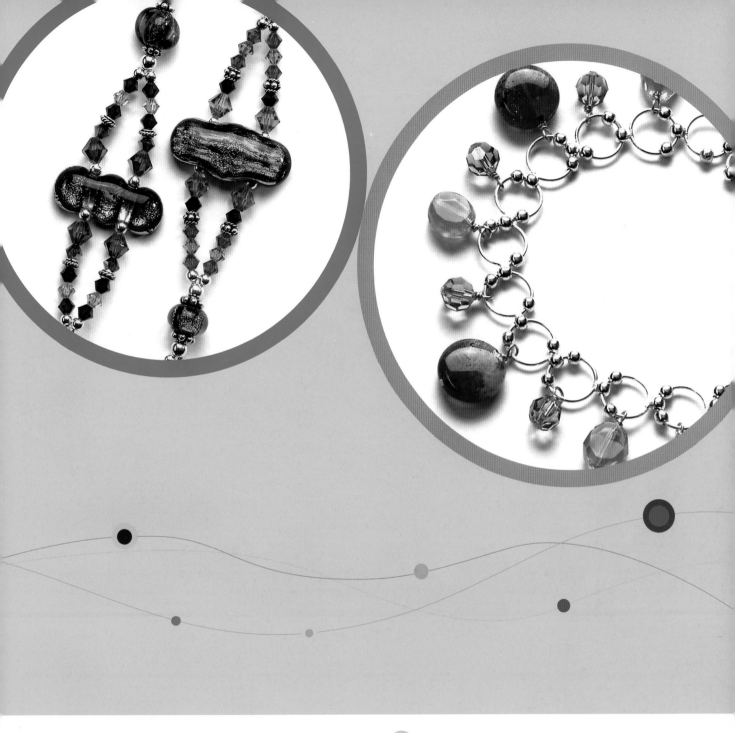

ceramic

by Karen Meyer

Artistic license

Art-glass beads dazzle at the forefront of a colorful necklace

1 necklace • Determine the finished length of your necklace. (This one is 15½ in./39.4cm.) Add 6 in. (15cm) and cut a piece of beading wire to that length. String: accent bead, flat spacer, art-glass bead, flat spacer, accent bead. Center the beads on the wire.

2 On each end, string a flat spacer, an art bead, a flat spacer, and an accent bead. Repeat twice, then string a flat spacer.

3 On each end, string rondelles until the necklace is within 2 in. (5cm) of the desired length.

EDITOR'S TIP
To maintain a balance between the focal beads and the rondelles, keep the necklace at choker length. Use two styles of art beads and arrange them in a symmetrical pattern.

How do you make the most of a few precious art-glass beads? Create impact by putting them at the front of the necklace. First, select gemstones to match a secondary color in the focal beads. In this version, pale amethyst rondelles bring out the lavender hues in the red and orange glass beads. Also consider combining textures: Nubby silver beads, vermeil spacers, and faceted rondelles contrast with the smooth glass. Go ahead and take some liberties; mix metals, textures, and colors.

SupplyList

necklace
- **7** 12–13mm art-glass beads (lampworked beads by Karen Meyer, karenbeads.com)
- 16-in. (41cm) strand 6 x 10mm faceted rondelles
- **8** 6mm accent beads
- **16** 6mm flat spacers
- **4** 3mm round spacers
- flexible beading wire, .014 or .015
- **2** crimp beads
- hook-and-eye clasp, or hook clasp and soldered jump ring
- chainnose or crimping pliers
- diagonal wire cutters

earrings
- **2** 12–13mm art-glass beads (Karen Meyer)
- **2** 6 x 10mm faceted rondelles
- **4** 6mm flat spacers
- **4** 3mm round spacers
- **2** 1½-in. (3.8cm) 20-gauge decorative head pins
- pair of earring wires
- chainnose pliers
- roundnose pliers
- diagonal wire cutters

4 On one end, string a round spacer, a crimp bead, a round spacer, and the hook half of the clasp. Go back through the last beads strung and tighten the wire. Repeat on the other end, substituting the eye half of the clasp or a jump ring for the hook. Check the fit, and add or remove beads from each end if necessary. Crimp the crimp beads (see Basics, p. 12), and trim the excess wire.

1 earrings • On a decorative head pin, string: round spacer, flat spacer, art-glass bead, flat spacer, rondelle, round spacer. Make a plain loop (Basics) above the spacer.

2 Open the loop of an earring wire. Attach the dangle and close the loop. Make a second earring to match the first. ❖

HIGH-BEAM
bracelet

Richly colored dichroic glass and crystals
turn on the brights • **by Karen Gollhardt**

A dichroic-glass focal bead delivers twice the impact
when strung with a double band of crystals. Choose
crystals that mimic the saturated colors in your focal
bead. Add dichroic accent beads on each side for jewelry
that shines on high.

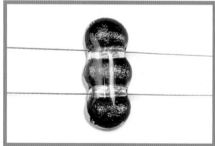

1 Determine the finished length of
your bracelet, add 5 in. (13cm), and
cut two pieces of beading wire to that
length. String a double-drilled dichroic
focal bead over both wires.

2 On each end of each wire, string a
3mm round spacer, a 6mm bicone
crystal, a color A 4mm bicone crystal,
and a 4mm flat spacer.

3 On each end of each wire, string a
color B 4mm bicone crystal, a color
C 4mm bicone crystal, a color B crystal,
and a 3mm spacer.

4 On each side, over both wires,
string: 4mm round spacer, 5mm flat
spacer, dichroic accent bead, 5mm flat
spacer, 4mm round spacer.

5 On each end of each wire, string: 3mm spacer, color B crystal, color C crystal, 4mm flat spacer, color C crystal, color B crystal, 3mm spacer.

SUPPLY NOTES
• The rectangular double-drilled focal beads are available from Sarah Creekmore Glass, (505) 854-2912, sararuna.com; or from Karen Gollhardt, (847) 981-1159, karilyndesigns@yahoo.com.
• The orange dichroic lampworked beads can be purchased from Midnight Moon Beads, (608) 877-1577, midnightmoon.biz. The violet dichroic accent beads are made by Paula Radke, info@paularadke.com.

6 a Open a jump ring (see Basics, p. 12). Attach half of the clasp and a soldered jump ring. Close the jump ring. Repeat with the remaining half of the clasp.

b On each side, over both wires, string a 4mm round spacer, a crimp bead, a 4mm round spacer, and the soldered jump ring with the clasp half attached. Go back through the beads just strung and tighten the wires. Check the fit, and add or remove beads from each end if necessary. Crimp the crimp beads (Basics) and trim the excess wire. ✿

Supply List

• 15 x 26mm rectangular double-drilled dichroic-glass focal bead
• 2 10mm or larger dichroic-glass accent beads
• 4 6mm bicone crystals
• **32 or more** 4mm bicone crystals: 4 color A, **16** color B, **12** color C
• 4 5mm flat spacers
• 8 4mm flat spacers
• 8 4mm round spacers
• 16 3mm round spacers
• flexible beading wire, .014 or .015
• 2 3–4mm soldered jump rings
• 2 3–4mm jump rings
• **2** crimp beads
• toggle clasp
• 2 pairs of chainnose pliers, or chainnose and roundnose pliers
• crimping pliers (optional)
• diagonal wire cutters

Create colorful
ornaments with
unusual glass beads

by Naomi Fujimoto

A few of our

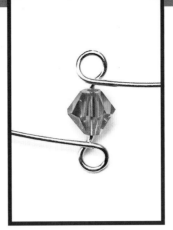

1 **pillow ornament**
To make a glass bead unit, cut a 4-in. (10cm) piece of wire. Make a wrapped loop (see Basics, p. 12) at one end. String a glass bead, crystals, and spacers as desired. Make a wrapped loop above the top bead.

2 To make a crystal unit, cut a 2-in. (5cm) piece of wire. Make the first half of a wrapped loop at one end. String a crystal and make the first half of a wrapped loop at the other end.

3 To make a dangle, string crystals and spacers on a head pin, or on a spiral, as desired. (To make a spiral, follow step 2 of the round-ornament instructions.) Make the first half of a wrapped loop above the top bead.

4 Attach the dangle's loop to the bottom loop of the glass-bead unit. Complete the wraps.

5 Attach a loop on the crystal unit to the top loop on the glass-bead unit. Cut a 5½-in. (14cm) piece of chain. Attach each end to the crystal unit's top loop. Complete the top and bottom wraps.

Candy-sized pillows

And icicles bright,

Egg-shaped and round glass

That sparkle with light

Ornaments that take

Just moments to string,

These are a few of

Our holiday things.

favorite things

SupplyList

all projects
- chainnose pliers
- roundnose pliers
- diagonal wire cutters

pillow ornament
- 1-in. (2.5cm) glass pillow bead (Olive Glass, oliveglass.com)
- **4 or more** 4–7mm crystals
- **2 or more** 4–5mm spacers
- 6–9 in. (15–23cm) 24-gauge craft or gold-filled wire
- 5½ in. (14cm) chain, 3mm or larger links
- 1½-in. (3.8cm) decorative head pin (optional)

squiggle ornament
- glass squiggle bead, approximately 3 in. (7.6cm) long (Olive Glass)
- **4–8** 3–8mm crystals
- **1–4** 3–6mm spacers
- 12–15 in. (30–38cm) 24-gauge craft or gold-filled wire

- 5½ in. (14cm) chain, 3mm or larger links
- 2-in. (5cm) decorative head pin (optional)
- twisted-wire beading needle

egg-shaped ornament
- egg-shaped blown glass bead, approximately 20 x 24mm (Olive Glass)
- 8mm round crystal
- 6mm round crystal
- 7mm spacer
- 2½ in. (6.4cm) 20-gauge craft or gold-filled wire, or 2½-in. (6.4cm) eye pin
- 7 in. (18cm) chain, 3mm or larger links

round ornament
- 30mm round glass bead (Olive Glass)
- **7–12** 3–8mm crystals
- **1–4** 3–6mm spacers
- 9 in. (23cm) 24-gauge craft or gold-filled wire
- 5½ in. (14cm) chain, 3mm or larger links

1 squiggle ornament
Cut a 10-in. (25cm) piece of wire. Gently pass the wire through the glass bead (see Design Guidelines, p. 23). Make a wrapped loop (Basics) at each end.

2 Follow steps 2 and 3 of the pillow ornament. Attach the crystal unit, the dangle, and a chain as in steps 4 and 5.

1 egg-shaped ornament
Cut a 2½-in. (6.4cm) piece of wire and make a plain loop (Basics) at one end; or, use an eye pin. To make a glass-bead unit, string an 8mm crystal, a glass bead, a spacer, and a 6mm crystal on the eye pin. Make a plain loop above the top bead.

2 Cut a 1-in. (2.5cm) piece of chain. Open the bottom loop of the glass-bead unit and attach the chain. Close the loop.

3 Cut a 5½-in. piece of chain. Open the top loop of the glass-bead unit and attach each end of the chain. Close the loop.

Design Guidelines

• Use craft or gold-filled wire. Avoid sterling-silver wire, which will tarnish in storage.

• Select tarnish-resistant chain and spacers. Chain from thrift-store jewelry works well and is inexpensive.

• To string wire through a squiggle-shaped bead: String the wire through the eye of a twisted-wire beading needle. Make a fold in the wire about an inch (2.5cm) from the end. Pass the needle through the bead, pushing the wire from the other end as necessary.

• Consider the size of the area you want to decorate. The pillows' small size makes them ideal for tabletop trees, while squiggles enhance window space, mantels, or bigger trees.

1 round ornament • Cut a 4-in. piece of wire. Make a wrapped loop (Basics) at one end. String the glass bead, crystals, and spacers as desired. Make a wrapped loop above the top bead.

2 To make a spiral, cut a 3-in. (7.6cm) piece of wire and make a loop at one end. Position chainnose pliers across the loop to hold it in place. Using your fingers, coil the wire into a spiral, then bend the wire upward. String beads as desired. Make the first half of a wrapped loop above the top bead.

3 Make a crystal unit as in step 2 of the pillow-ornament instructions. Attach the spiral, the crystal unit, and the chain as in steps 4 and 5. ❖

Nothing if knot ver

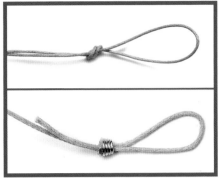

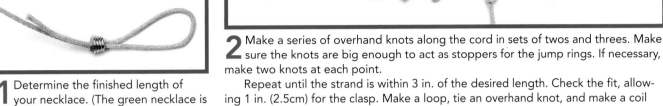

1 Determine the finished length of your necklace. (The green necklace is 16 in./41cm; the black necklace, 24 in./61cm.) Cut a piece of cord to triple the finished length.

Fold the cord, leaving a ¾-in. (1.9cm) loop. Tie an overhand knot (see Basics, p. 12). Glue the knot. Cut a 3-in. (7.6cm) piece of wire. Tightly coil it around the knot. Trim the excess cord.

2 Make a series of overhand knots along the cord in sets of twos and threes. Make sure the knots are big enough to act as stoppers for the jump rings. If necessary, make two knots at each point.

Repeat until the strand is within 3 in. of the desired length. Check the fit, allowing 1 in. (2.5cm) for the clasp. Make a loop, tie an overhand knot, and make a coil around the knot as in step 1.

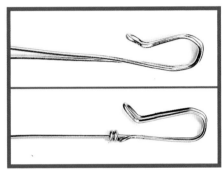

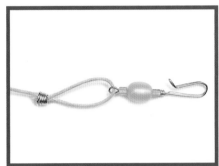

3 **a** Cut a 4-in. (10cm) piece of wire. Fold it in half. Using roundnose pliers, bend the wire into a hook.

b Wrap one wire around the other near the base of the hook. Trim the excess wrapping wire.

4 String three beads on the wire stem and make a plain loop (Basics) on the stem next to the last bead.

Open the loop and attach one end of the cord. Close the loop.

by Linda Jones

This necklace can be created with cotton cord, ribbon, leather, or suede. It can be lengthened for a belt or shortened for a bracelet. The hook clasp can fasten anywhere, with the bead tassel in front or back. You have a lot of choices to make, so grab your favorite beads and start knotting.

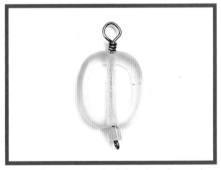

5 Determine the total number of dangles. You'll need one or two fewer dangles than the number of knots, plus eight for the tassel.

Make about one-third of the dangles with coil ends. For each, cut a 3-in. piece of wire and make a small coil on one end with roundnose pliers. String an 8º or 11º seed bead and a glass bead. Make a wrapped loop (Basics) above the top bead.

6 Make one-third of the dangles with loop ends. For each, cut a 3-in. piece of wire and make a small loop at one end with roundnose pliers. String an 8º or 11º and a glass bead. Make a wrapped loop above the top bead.

satile

A clever design comes with many variations

7 Make one-third of the dangles with decorative wire wraps. For each, cut a 4-in. piece of wire. Bend it in half and string a glass bead. Wrap one wire end around the bead. Make a set of wraps above the bead.

Make a wrapped loop above the wraps. Trim the excess wire.

SupplyList

- **24–40** 6–20mm glass beads in assorted shapes
- 2g 8º or 11º seed beads
- 4–6 ft. (1.2–1.8m) cotton cord
- 8–12 ft. (2.4–3.7m) 24-gauge half-hard wire
- **4** 5–8mm jump rings
- **16–32** 5mm jump rings
- chainnose pliers
- roundnose pliers
- diagonal wire cutters
- E6000 adhesive

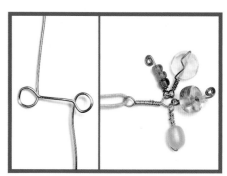

8 To make a coil dangle, cut a 1½-in. (3.8cm) piece of wire and make a loop on one end. String 1 in. of 8ºs or 11ºs. Make a loop above the top bead.

Using your fingers, shape the bead unit into a coil.

9 **a** Cut a 3-in. piece of wire. Leaving ½ in. (1.3cm) of wire in the center, make the first half of a wrapped loop on each end.

b Attach the remaining cord loop to one end and four dangles to the other. Complete the wraps.

EDITOR'S TIP
Use niobium wire to add another colorful design dimension.

10 Open a jump ring (Basics). Attach two dangles and the wrapped-loop end. Close the jump ring. Use jump rings to attach several dangles as desired.

11 Using a jump ring, attach a dangle to the cord between the end loop and the first knot. Close the jump ring. Using jump rings, attach one or two dangles between each knot. ❖

by **Maria Camera**

Quick pick

Save time by attaching beads to a premade chain bracelet

Streamline the task of selecting materials by starting with a finished chain bracelet. Then add bead dangles in round shapes: lentils, curvy nuggets, and crystals. Prefab can be pretty fabulous.

Supply List

- **4** 12mm lentil beads
- **4** 9–11mm glass nuggets
- **8** 6mm round crystals
- 7-in. (18cm) beaded 9.3mm round-link bracelet (Rio Grande, 800-545-6566)
- **16** 1½-in. (3.8cm) head pins
- lobster claw clasp and soldered jump ring (optional)
- **2** 4mm jump rings (optional)
- chainnose pliers
- roundnose pliers
- diagonal wire cutters

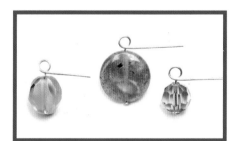

1 String a glass nugget on a head pin. Make the first half of a wrapped loop (see Basics, p. 12) above the bead. Repeat with the remaining beads for a total of four nugget units, four lentil units, and eight crystal units.

2 Attach the loop of a nugget unit to an end link of the bracelet's chain. On the next link, attach a crystal unit. Attach a lentil unit to the next link and a crystal unit to the next. Complete the wraps. Repeat the pattern three times.

3 Check the fit. To lengthen the bracelet, remove the spring clasp. Use a jump ring (Basics) to attach a lobster claw clasp to one end and a soldered jump ring to the other end. Or, attach additional jump rings to each end. To shorten the bracelet, trim links and reattach the spring clasp with a jump ring. ✤

Wrapped

by Stacie Thompson

Frame focal beads with gleaming wire for fabulous earrings

Paying attention to the tiniest detail can make the difference between just a nice set of earrings and something truly remarkable. The subtle metal cradle created by wrapping a thin wire around the perimeter of a flat bead gives a gleam of sophistication to the simplest of styles.

attention

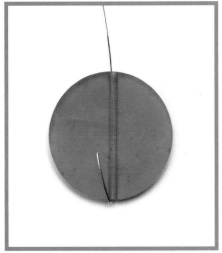

1 Cut a 12-in. (30cm) piece of wire. String a flat bead. Bend ¼ in. (6mm) of wire up at the bottom of the bead.

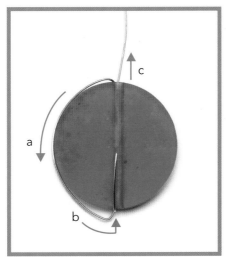

2 Wrap the wire down and around one side of the bead and up through the bottom hole so the working end of the wire comes back through the top of the bead. Pull the wire taut while shaping it against the side of the bead.

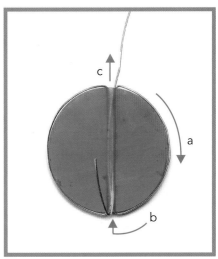

3 Repeat step 2 on the other side of the bead.

4 String three beads. Pull the wire taut, and make a wrapped loop (see Basics, p. 12) above the top bead. Trim the ¼-in. wire hook at the bottom of the bead as close to the hole as possible.

5 Open the loop on an earring wire. Attach the dangle and close the loop. Make a second earring to match the first. ❖

SupplyList

- **2** 15–35mm large-hole flat beads
- **6** 4–9mm beads in 2 or 3 shapes
- **2** ft. (61cm) 26-gauge half-hard wire
- pair of earring wires
- chainnose pliers
- roundnose pliers
- diagonal wire cutters

EDITOR'S TIPS

- Make sure your flat beads have a hole that is large enough to allow the wire to pass through three times.
- Instead of cutting off the ¼-in. wire hook in step 4, make a small decorative spiral.

The village of Krobo in Ghana, Africa, makes beads by hand from reclaimed and recycled glass. The process is painstaking, and occasionally a bit dangerous. Shards are crushed against a flat stone, mixed with pigments, poured into molds, fired in a wood-fired kiln, and hand-painted. The result of the artisans' five-day process is an eclectic collection of colorful beads that can be worn alone or combined with classic materials. For more details on the Krobo beadmaking process or to purchase beads, visit anansevillage.com. Ananse Village is a member of the Fair Trade Federation.

by Cathy Jakicic

Working glass heroes

String a bright necklace of glass beads

1 **blue necklace** • Determine the finished length of your necklace. (This one is 18½ in./47cm.) Add 6 in. (15cm) and cut a piece of beading wire to that length. String a round spacer, a crimp bead, and the clasp. Go back through the beads just strung and tighten the wire. Crimp the crimp bead (see Basics, p. 12), and trim the excess wire, leaving a tail to tuck under the next bead strung.

2 String a button pearl, a spacer, a pearl, and a tube bead. Repeat the pattern until the strand is within 1 in. (2.5cm) of the desired length. End with a pearl, a spacer, and a pearl.

3 String a spacer, a crimp bead, and the jump ring. Go back through the beads just strung and tighten the wire. Check the fit, and add or remove beads if necessary. Crimp the crimp bead, and trim the excess wire.

1 **black-and-white necklace** • Determine the finished length of your necklace. (This one is 18½ in.) Add 6 in. and cut a piece of beading wire to that length. On the wire, center: saucer spacer, two pearls, spacer, tube bead, spacer, two pearls, spacer. On each side, string a tube bead and a pearl; repeat until the strand is within 2 in. (5cm) of the desired length.

2 On one end, string a spacer, a crimp bead, a spacer, and the clasp. Go back through the beads just strung and tighten the wires. Repeat on the other end, substituting a jump ring for the clasp. Crimp the crimp beads, and trim the excess wire.

1 **bracelet** • Determine the finished length of your bracelet, add 5 in. (13cm), and cut a piece of beading wire to that length. String a crimp bead, a round crystal, and the clasp. Go back through the beads just strung. Tighten the wire, and crimp the crimp bead. Trim the excess wire, leaving a tail to tuck under the next few beads strung.

2 String: crystal, top-drilled pearl, crystal, two disk beads, pearl, two disk beads. Repeat the pattern until the strand is within 1 in. of the desired length. End with a crystal, a pearl, and a crystal.

3 String a crimp bead, a crystal, and the jump ring. Go back through the last few beads strung. Check the fit, and add or remove beads if necessary. Crimp the crimp bead, and trim the excess wire. ❖

EDITOR'S NOTE
This project was designed with beads that are a major source of income for the community that makes them. For many of us, wearing beautiful beads makes us feel beautiful. These Beads of Change beads are not only beautiful, but also powerful: They enrich the lives of those who work together to make them and those who make the choice to buy them. Look for other Beads of Change projects throughout this book.

Supply List

all projects
• chainnose or crimping pliers
• diagonal wire cutters
• flexible beading wire, .014 or .015

blue necklace
• 20-bead strand Krobo tube beads
• **23–27** 6mm round spacers
• **42–50** 4mm button pearls
• **2** crimp beads
• lobster claw clasp and soldered jump ring

black-and-white necklace
• 16-bead strand, Krobo tube beads
• **16** 12mm round pearls
• **8** 6mm saucer spacers
• **2** crimp beads
• lobster claw clasp and soldered jump ring

bracelet
• 84-bead strand, Krobo disk beads
• **10–12** 8mm top-drilled pearls
• **14–16** 4mm round crystals
• **2** crimp beads
• lobster claw clasp and soldered jump ring

by Helene Tsigistras

Desert-sun beads are made of clear glass that has been coated in gold or silver plating and fired. Then, the beads are coated with color and refired, shrinking the color coating away from the plating to form fissures. Complement these metallic tones with round, cylinder, and oval metal beads for a texture-rich trio.

Spread some sunshine with a necklace, bracelet, and earrings strung with gold-plated beads

Textured trio

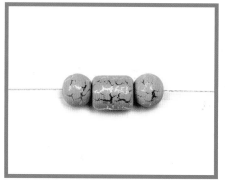

1 necklace • Determine the finished length of your necklace. (The peach necklace is 15 in./38cm; the blue, 18 in./46cm.) Add 6 in. (15cm), and cut a piece of beading wire to that length. String: shape A metal bead, bead cap, desert-sun oval bead, bead cap, shape B metal bead, shape C metal bead, shape B metal bead. Center the beads on the wire.

2 On each end, string a desert-sun round bead, a desert-sun cylinder, and a round.

3 a On one end, string the pattern in step 1. On the other end, string the pattern in reverse. Repeat step 2.

b Repeat step 3a until the strand is within 2 in. (5cm) of the desired length. End with a metal bead.

4 On each end, string a crimp bead, a metal bead, and half of the clasp. Go back through the last beads strung and tighten the wires. Check the fit, and add or remove beads from each end if necessary. Crimp the crimp beads (see Basics, p. 12). Trim the excess wire.

SUPPLY NOTES

• Desert-sun beads are sold in 16-in. (41cm) strands. Two strands are enough for a necklace, bracelet, and earrings.

• Beads for this project are available at Fire Mountain Gems, (800) 355-2137, firemountaingems.com.

bracelet • Determine the finished length of your bracelet, add 5 in. (13cm), and cut a piece of beading wire to that length.

String: shape A metal bead, bead cap, desert-sun cylinder bead, bead cap, shape B metal bead. Repeat this pattern until the strand is within 1 in. (2.5cm) of the desired length.

Repeat step 4 of the necklace to finish.

SupplyList

necklace

- **4–6** 16–18mm desert-sun oval beads
- **3–5** 10mm desert-sun cylinder beads
- **6–10** 8mm desert-sun round beads
- **20–30** 8–12mm metal beads: **6–8** shape A, **8–14** shape B, **6–8** shape C
- **10–14** 10mm bead caps
- flexible beading wire, .014 or .015
- **2** crimp beads
- toggle clasp
- chainnose or crimping pliers
- diagonal wire cutters

bracelet

- **4–6** 10mm desert-sun cylinder beads
- **10–14** 8–12mm metal beads: **5–7** shape A, **5–7** shape B
- **8–12** 10mm bead caps
- flexible beading wire, .014 or .015
- **2** crimp beads
- toggle clasp
- chainnose or crimping pliers
- diagonal wire cutters

earrings

- **2** 8–10mm desert-sun round beads
- **2** 4mm spacers
- **1** in. (2.5cm) cable chain, 3mm links
- **2** 1½-in. (3.8cm) head pins
- pair of earring wires
- chainnose pliers
- roundnose pliers
- diagonal wire cutters

1 earrings • To make a bead unit, string a spacer and a desert-sun round bead on a head pin. Make the first half of a wrapped loop (Basics).

2 Cut a ½-in. (1.3cm) piece of chain. Attach the bead unit to the chain. Complete the wraps.

3 Open the loop on an earring wire and attach the dangle. Close the loop. Make a second earring to match the first. ❧

Well rounded

String easy hoop earrings in an array of bright colors

by Maria Camera

Round out your wardrobe with a perennial favorite. Hoop earrings add a finishing touch with dainty crystal briolettes and seed beads. Universally flattering, they're a top pick for no-fuss accessorizing.

SupplyList

- **14** briolettes, approximately 6 x 10mm
- 1g 8º hex-cut seed beads
- 1g 11º seed beads
- 9 in. (23cm) 22-gauge half-hard wire
- **2** crimp beads
- chainnose pliers
- roundnose pliers
- diagonal wire cutters
- metal file or emery board
- 35mm-film canister or other round object

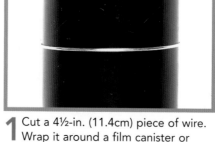

1 Cut a 4½-in. (11.4cm) piece of wire. Wrap it around a film canister or other round object.

2 String an alternating pattern of seven briolettes and 11º seed beads. Center the beads on the wire.

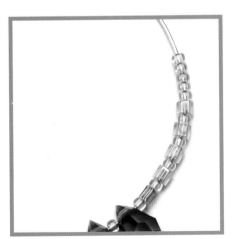

3 On each end, string an alternating pattern of five 11º and five 8º seed beads. String five 11ºs.

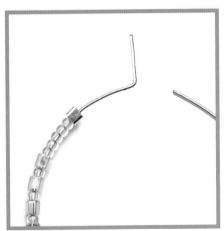

4 On one end, string a crimp bead and crimp it (see Basics, p. 12). Approximately ½ in. (1.3cm) from the end, bend the wire up. File the end.

5 On the other end, trim the excess wire to ¼ in. (6mm) and make a plain loop (Basics). ❖

Create a graduated five-strand
necklace with perfect alignment

by Anne Nikolai Kloss

Dramatic drape

The smooth drape and clean lines of this multistrand
necklace are created by careful alignment of bead
sections. There are two ways to ensure uniform bead
spacing: Count the number of beads, or measure the
length strung. Japanese seed beads are consistently sized,
so you can count beads for accurate measurements.
Czech seed beads are irregular in size, so measuring
rows is necessary. With either method, a multichannel
design board is a great aid for aligning the bead strands.
Because the channels are curved, each strand will be in
proportion, giving the necklace an even, graceful drape.

EDITOR'S TIP
Crimp the crimp beads while the
necklace is in a curved position to
allow each strand to drape.
Crimping when the strands are
straight crowds the beads.

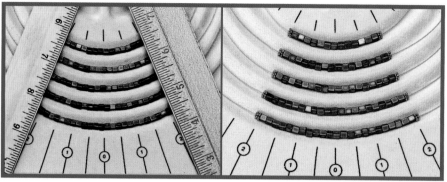

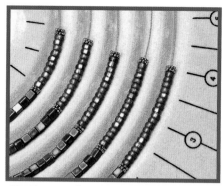

1 a Determine the finished length of your necklace. (The strands in the burgundy necklace range from 19–26 in./48–66cm; the strands in the blue necklace, 17–24 in./43–61cm.) Add 6 in. (15cm) to the shortest measurement, and cut a piece of beading wire to that length. Cut four more pieces, each 2 in. (5cm) longer than the previous wire.

b Align a ruler along each 2-in. mark on the design board. String cubes on the shortest wire, filling in the design board's top channel between the rulers. String cubes on each successive wire; the longest wire will have the most cubes.

c String two flat spacers on each end of each wire.

2 Align a ruler along each 4-in. (10cm) mark on the design board. String matte beads on each end of each strand, filling in the channels between the rulers. String two flat spacers on each end of each strand.

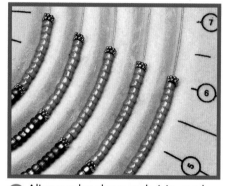

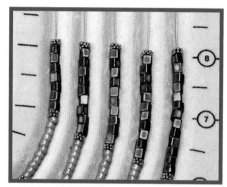

3 Align a ruler along each 6-in. mark on the design board. String silver-lined beads on each end of each strand, filling in the channels between the rulers. String two flat spacers on each end of each strand.

4 Align a ruler along each 8-in. (20cm) mark on the design board. String cubes on each end of each strand, filling in the channels between the rulers. String two flat spacers on each end of each strand.

5 String 2 in. of matte beads on each end of each strand. On each end, string the respective hole of a five-strand spacer bar.

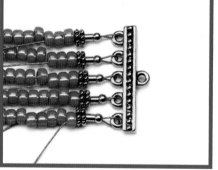

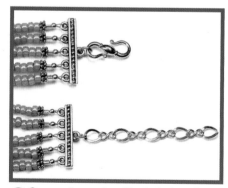

6 String 2 in. of silver-lined beads on each end of the shortest strand. On the next strand, string that amount plus one bead. On the remaining strands, string one bead more than on the previous strand. String two flat spacers on each end of each strand.

7 On each strand, string a crimp bead, a round spacer, and the respective loop of a connector bar. Go back through the beads just strung plus a few more and tighten the wires. Check the fit, and add or remove an equal number of beads from each end if necessary. Crimp the crimp beads (see Basics, p. 12), and trim the excess wire.

8 Open a jump ring (Basics). Attach one connector bar's loop and the clasp. Close the jump ring.

Cut a 2-in. piece of chain. Open a jump ring and attach the chain and the remaining connector bar's loop. Close the jump ring. ❖

SupplyList

- 60g 6º or 8º seed beads, 30g each of matte and another type (such as silver-lined)
- 30g 4mm Japanese cube beads
- **2** 6 x 27mm five-strand spacer bars
- **2** 10 x 27mm five-to-one connector bars
- **100** 4mm flat spacers
- **10** 3mm round spacers
- flexible beading wire, .014 or .015
- **2** 5mm jump rings
- **10** crimp beads
- S-hook clasp
- 2 in. (5cm) chain, 4–5mm links
- chainnose or crimping pliers
- diagonal wire cutters
- **2** rulers
- five-channel design board

Curtain call

Create light-catching accents for your favorite window

When you're pulling the curtain back to let the sun shine in, make sure those rays have something to catch with these colorful tiebacks. The lariat is adjustable to suit the sheerest draperies, while the memory-wire version is perfect for thicker fabrics.

by Steven James

1 **lariat tieback** • String a spacer and an oval bead on a head pin. Make a wrapped loop (see Basics, p. 12).

3 String a crimp bead and the loop of the oval-bead unit. Go back through the last few beads strung. Crimp the crimp bead (Basics) and trim the excess wire.

2 Determine the finished length of your tieback. (This one is 45 in./1.1m.) Add 6 in. (15cm), and cut a piece of beading wire to that length. Tape the end and string 2 in. (5cm) of seed beads. String a crimp bead, and then continue stringing seed beads until the strand is 2 in. longer than the desired length.

4 Remove the tape from the other end. Form a loop by pulling the wire through the crimp bead and the two adjacent beads. Crimp the crimp bead, and trim the excess wire.

5 On each end, gently close a crimp cover over the crimp bead with chainnose or crimping pliers.

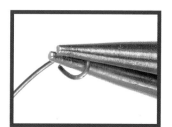

1 a **memory-wire tieback** Separate four coils of memory wire from the stack of coils. Hold the wire with chainnose pliers and bend it back and forth at one place until the wire breaks. You also can use heavy-duty wire cutters. (Do not use jewelry-weight cutters.) Make a small loop at one end of the wire using roundnose pliers.
b String seed beads until ½ in. (1.3cm) of the coil remains. Make a loop at the end.

2 a To make the tassels, determine the desired length. (These are 3 in./ 7.6cm). Double that measurement, and cut five pieces of beading wire to that length.
b String a crimp bead and three seed beads. Go back through the three seed beads and tighten the wire. Crimp the crimp bead (Basics) and trim the excess wire. String beads to the desired length.

3 a String a crimp bead and one of the memory-wire loops. Go back through the last four beads strung. Crimp the crimp bead and trim the excess wire. Place a crimp cover over each crimp bead and gently close it.
b Repeat steps 2b and 3a for a total of five tassels. Attach three to one memory-wire loop and two to the other. ❖

Seed bead

Multiple strands of seed beads take shape in an elegant necklace

by Susan Tobias

1 Determine the finished length of your necklace. (These are 19½ in./49.5cm.) Add 6 in. (15cm) and cut six pieces of beading wire to that length. Center a crimp bead on all six wires. Crimp the crimp bead (see Basics, p. 12). Center the large tube bead over the crimp. On each side, over all six wires, string a bicone crystal and a crimp bead. Crimp the crimp beads.

2 On each side, over all six wires, string two bead caps so the narrow ends meet.

3 On each side, on each wire, string approximately 3 in. (7.6cm) of 11º seed beads.

44

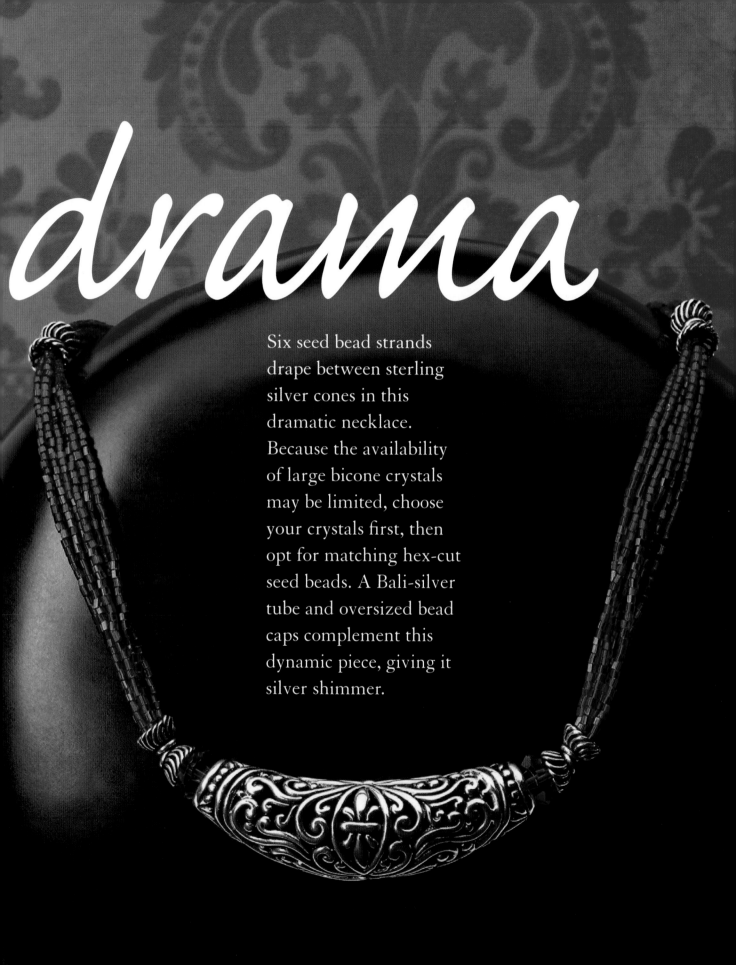

drama

Six seed bead strands drape between sterling silver cones in this dramatic necklace. Because the availability of large bicone crystals may be limited, choose your crystals first, then opt for matching hex-cut seed beads. A Bali-silver tube and oversized bead caps complement this dynamic piece, giving it silver shimmer.

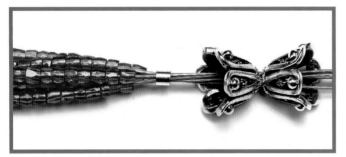

4 On each side, over all six wires, string a crimp bead and crimp it. Repeat steps 2 and 3. Check the fit, allowing 3 in. (7.6cm) for finishing. Add or remove beads if necessary. String a crimp bead, crimp it, and repeat step 2 again.

5 On each side, over all six wires, string a bicone, a crimp bead, a bead cap, and half of the clasp. Go back through the beads just strung and tighten the wires. Crimp the crimp beads, and trim the excess wire. ❖

EDITOR'S TIP
Rather than stringing tiny seed beads individually, transfer them directly from the hank onto your beading wire. String your beading wire through the seed beads while they are still strung on the hank. Then pull out the hank string.

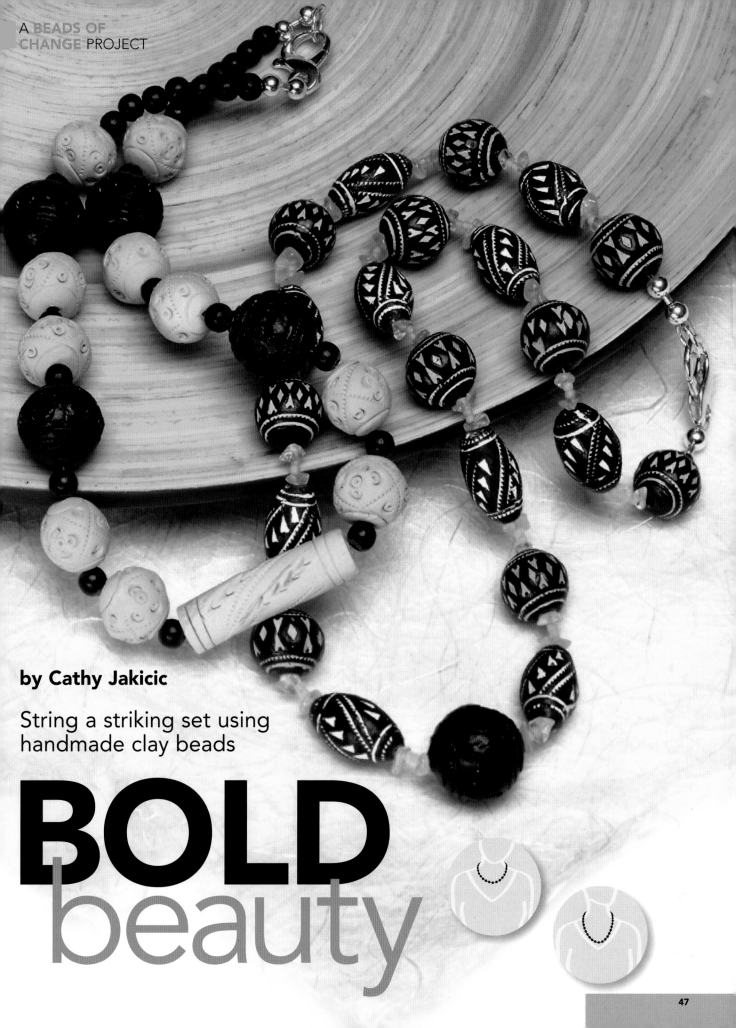

by Cathy Jakicic

String a striking set using
handmade clay beads

BOLD
beauty

The craftswomen of the northeastern Thailand region, often called Esarn, have been making clay beads for 600 years. Many residents of the Esarn villages are adept at various utilitarian and decorative arts in an area where the agriculture produces little above subsistence level. Each bead is made by hand and is sold in the villages, usually directly by the artisan or group that made them. The beads are made from native clay – one piece at a time – and fired in backyard kilns. Occasionally, they will bear the faint fingerprint of the artist who created them.

1 green/black necklace • Determine the finished length of your necklace. (This one is 18 in./46cm.) Add 6 in. (15cm) and cut a piece of beading wire to that length. Center a tube bead on the wire.

2 On each end, string: 6mm round bead, 15mm round bead, 6mm, 15mm, 6mm, 20mm round bead. Repeat the pattern on each end.

3 On each end, string a 6mm and a 15mm. String 6mms until the strand is within 2 in. (5cm) of the desired length.

On one end, string a spacer, a crimp bead, a spacer, and a lobster claw clasp. Go back through the beads just strung and tighten the wire. Repeat on the other end, substituting a soldered jump ring for the clasp. Check the fit, and add or remove beads from each end if necessary. Crimp the crimp beads (see Basics, p. 12), and trim the excess wire.

1 pink/black necklace • Determine the finished length of your necklace. (This one is 22 in./56cm.) Add 6 in., and cut a piece of beading wire to that length. Center a 20mm round bead on the wire.

2 On each end, string: gemstone chip, two 11º seed beads, chip, oval bead, chip, two 11ºs, chip, 15mm round bead. Repeat the pattern until the strand is within 2 in. of the desired length.

3 On one end, string a spacer, a crimp bead, a spacer, and a lobster claw clasp. Go back through the beads just strung and tighten the wire. Repeat on the other end, substituting a soldered jump ring for the clasp. Check the fit, and add or remove beads from each end if necessary. Crimp the crimp beads, and trim the excess wire.

EDITOR'S TIPS

• Make multiple bracelets to wear together. The individuality of each terra-cotta bead is accentuated when they're seen next to each other.
• Quantities of handmade beads are finite, so be prepared to be flexible when shopping. The good news is that many more beautiful designs are available than we could show here.

SUPPLY NOTE

The handmade terra-cotta beads for these projects are available from Jewelry Supply Inc., (916) 780-9610, jewelrysupply.com.

1 bracelet • Determine the finished length of your bracelet. Add 5 in. (13cm), double the number, and cut a piece of ribbon elastic to that length. Double the elastic and string the tube bead.

String a 5mm round bead and six 6º seed beads. Repeat until the strand is the desired length.

2 Tie the ends together with a surgeon's knot (Basics). Trim the elastic, put a dot of G-S Hypo Cement on the knot, and tuck the knot into the tube bead. ❖

Supply List

green / black necklace
• 10 x 38mm terra-cotta tube bead
• 4 20mm round terra-cotta beads
• 10 15mm round terra-cotta beads
• 28–38 6mm round beads
• 4 5mm round spacers

• flexible beading wire, .014 or .015
• 2 crimp beads
• lobster claw clasp and soldered jump ring
• chainnose or crimping pliers
• diagonal wire cutters

pink / black necklace
• 20mm round terra-cotta bead
• 10 15mm round terra-cotta beads

• 10 12 x 20mm oval terra-cotta beads
• 40 gemstone chips
• 2g 11º seed beads
• 4 5mm round spacers
• flexible beading wire, .014 or .015
• 2 crimp beads
• lobster claw clasp and soldered jump ring
• chainnose or crimping pliers
• diagonal wire cutters

bracelet
• 9 x 36mm terra-cotta tube bead
• 6–10 5mm round beads
• 4g 6º seed beads
• ribbon elastic
• G-S Hypo Cement
• scissors

Small

Delicate links showcase Kenyan beads in this long necklace and earrings set

by Jane Konkel

Approximately 30 minutes from Nairobi lies a workshop where ceramic beads are shaped, polished, fired, painted, and refired. The result is "kazuri," the Swahili word for "small and beautiful." In 1975, philanthropist Lady Susan Wood established Kazuri Ltd. with the mission of providing work for a few women. Today, Kazuri employs 120 Kenyan women, most of whom provide for 10 to 20 extended family members. Although the women walk miles to work, they receive health insurance and school supplies and uniforms for their children, and they earn three to five times the national average wage. Visit kazuriamerica.com to learn more.

& **beautiful**

1 necklace • Determine the finished length of your necklace. (This one is 42 in./1.1m.) Divide that number by 3 and cut that many pieces of 3½-in. (8.9cm) long wire.

On one end of a wire, make a wrapped loop (see Basics, p. 12). String a 4mm spacer, a flat bead, and a spacer. Make a wrapped loop next to the spacer. Repeat with the remaining wires.

2 Open a jump ring (Basics) and attach two 6mm spacers. Close the jump ring. Use jump rings to attach four more spacers. Make a six-spacer segment for each bead unit.

Supply**List**

both projects
• **2** pairs of chainnose pliers, or chainnose and roundnose pliers
• diagonal wire cutters

necklace
• **12–16** 22mm flat ceramic beads (Kazuri West, kazuriwest.com)
• **16-in.** (41cm) strand 6mm large-hole spacers
• **24–32** 4mm spacers
• **42–56 in.** (1.1–1.4m) 22-gauge half-hard wire
• **84–112** 5mm oval jump rings

earrings
• **2** 22mm flat ceramic beads (Kazuri West)
• **6** 6mm large-hole spacers
• **4** 4mm spacers
• **2** 2-in. (5cm) head pins
• **6** 5mm oval jump rings
• pair of earring wires

3 Use a jump ring to attach a six-spacer segment to a loop of a bead unit. Repeat on the other side.

4 Continue attaching bead units and spacer segments until the necklace is the desired length. Check the fit, and add or remove spacers and bead units if necessary.

1 earrings • On a head pin, string a 4mm spacer, a flat bead, and a spacer. Make a plain loop (Basics) above the top spacer.

2 Make a three-spacer segment as in step 2 of the necklace. Use a jump ring to attach the bead unit's loop to the spacer segment.

3 Open the loop of an earring wire. Attach the dangle and close the loop. Make a second earring to match the first. ✤

Happy glaze

Ceramics take the stage in this fashionable necklace

by Paulette Biedenbender

Ceramic beads are the cornerstones of this eclectic mix. While complementary in color, the range of shapes and finishes makes the elements of this two-strand necklace a kinetic combination. Experiment with different materials to ensure that your necklace is a one-of-a-kind creation.

1 To make the pendant, string the following on a head pin: bicone crystal, ceramic bead, bicone, ceramic, bicone, spacer. Make a wrapped loop above the top bead (see Basics, p. 12).

EDITOR'S TIP
To complement the whimsical nature of this necklace, use irregularly shaped gemstones.

2 Determine the finished length of your necklace. (The short strand of this necklace is 16 in./41cm). Add 6 in. (15cm) and cut a piece of beading wire to that length. Cut a second piece 1 in. (2.5cm) longer.
   Center the pendant on the long wire. On each end, string a spacer, a bicone, eight gemstone drops, and a rectangle bead. String eight drops and a rectangle on each end.

3 On each end, string: spacer, bicone, ceramic, bicone, spacer, rectangle, eight drops. On each end, string a rectangle and eight drops, repeating this pattern until the strand is within 2 in. (5cm) of the desired length. Tape the ends.

4 Center the curved tube bead on the short wire. On each end, string: bicone, two rondelles, drop, two rectangles, spacer, three drops, spacer, two rectangles, drop, two rondelles.

5 On each end of the short strand, string: spacer, bicone, ceramic, bicone, spacer, two rondelles, drop, two rectangles, spacer, three drops, spacer, four rectangles, spacer.
   On each end, string two rectangles and a spacer. Repeat this pattern until the strand is within 2 in. of the desired length. Tape the ends.

6 On one end of both strands, remove the tape and string a spacer, a crimp bead, and a spacer. String half of the clasp and go back through the last beads strung on each wire. Tighten the wires.
   Repeat on the other side with the remaining half of the clasp. Check the fit, and add or remove beads from each end if necessary. Crimp the crimp beads (Basics), and trim the excess wire. ❖

SupplyList

- set of six ceramic beads (all ceramic beads available from Jangles, jangles.net)
- 60mm curved ceramic tube
- 16-in. (41cm) strand 6–8mm gemstone drops
- 16-in. (41cm) strand 5–7mm gemstone rondelles or heishis
- 16-in. strand 5–6mm gemstone rectangles
- **15–20** 6mm bicone crystals
- **31–35** 3mm round spacers
- flexible beading wire, 014. or .015

- 2-in. (5cm) 22-gauge head pin
- **4** crimp beads
- ceramic toggle clasp
- chainnose pliers
- roundnose pliers
- diagonal wire cutters
- crimping pliers (optional)

Shortcuts

Readers' tips to make your beading life easier

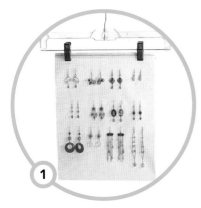

1 earring display
To make an inexpensive earring holder, attach a piece of needlepoint canvas to the clips on a pants hanger. Hook earrings through the holes in the canvas, and hang it in a closet for convenient storage. You'll be able to see all your earrings at a glance.
– *Cindy Klein, Tucson, Ariz.*

2 careful crimping
When finishing a strung bracelet with a lobster claw clasp and a jump ring, crimp the clasp end first. Fasten the clasp to the jump ring before crimping the other end. This will keep the jump ring away from the crimp bead. Finishing while the piece is in a curved shape will also ensure that the bracelet is not crimped too tightly.
– *R. Diamond, via e-mail*

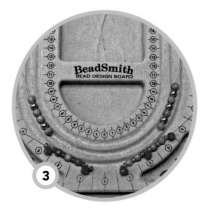

3 head pin arrangements
When designing a piece of jewelry, string combinations of beads and spacers on long head pins. Rearrange them on a bead-design board to see how the combinations look together. You'll save time when stringing different patterns and reorganizing groups of beads.
– *Marie Rankin, via e-mail*

4 tidy tote
Pick up a plastic organizer from your local home-improvement store. This one has four drawers with multiple compartments, a handle that folds down, and holes for wall mounting – all for only $10.
– *Ruth Zamarripa, Los Gatos, Calif.*

5 snack-tray convenience
Plastic snack trays make inexpensive project organizers. They have multiple compartments for storing beads, findings, and tools. Buy a bunch at a dollar or discount store.
– *T. L. Feingold, via e-mail*

6 spoon scoops
Tiny spoons make great scoops for tiny beads. Try a souvenir, demitasse, or baby spoon, or save the plastic spoons that come with artificial sweeteners or ice cream samples. They can get into the corners of a tray or design board for easy bead pickup, and also are handy for putting beads back in small containers or tubes.
– *Shawn Szilvasi, via e-mail, and Marlene Vidibor, Ghent, N.Y.*

Pearls

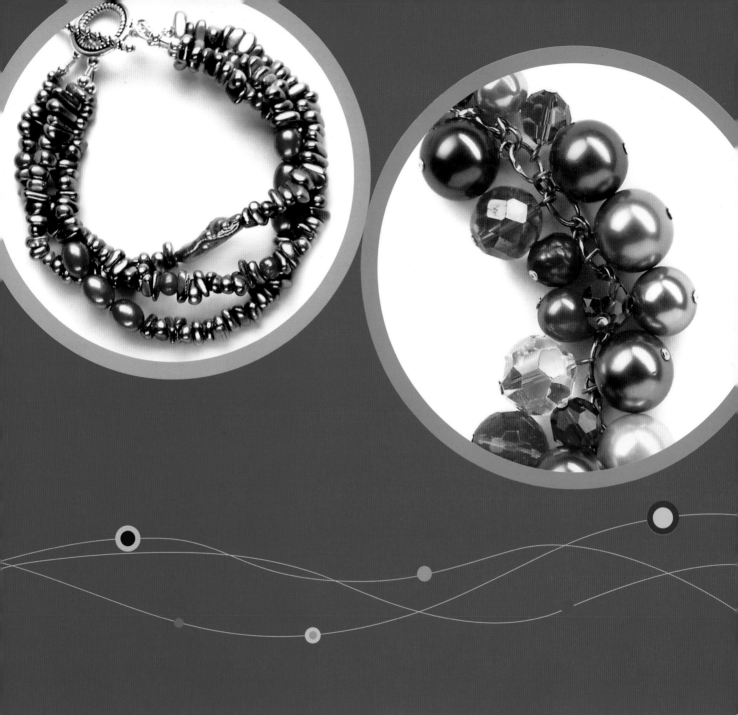

and shells

BIG
BANGLE
theory

Gumball-sized pearls are thrown into orbit in a fabulous bracelet and earrings

by Brenda Schweder

Ah, the bangled web we weave. Try to simplify and still make an impact by wearing one striking bangle. Here, round beads, square wire, and sterling loops come together to form a single stellar bracelet. The playful earrings hold asymmetrical pearl dangles suspended in space. Now your jewelry – if not your life – can be in perfect alignment.

Supply List

bracelet
- **14** 12 or 14mm round pearls
- **2** 3-in. (7.6cm) bangles with ruffled loop edges (Brenda Schweder, brendaschweder.com)
- 15–18 in. (38–46cm) 22-gauge half-hard square wire, sterling silver
- chainnose pliers
- roundnose pliers
- diagonal wire cutters

earrings
- **2** 12 or 14mm round pearls
- 11 in. (28cm) 22-gauge half-hard square wire, sterling silver
- pair of lever-back earring wires
- chainnose pliers
- roundnose pliers
- diagonal wire cutters

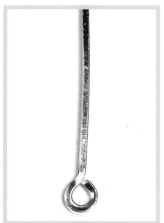

1 bracelet • If you're using 12mm pearls, cut 14 1¹⁄₁₆-in. (2.7cm) pieces of wire. For 14mm pearls, cut 14 1¼-in. (3.2cm) pieces of wire. Make a plain loop (see Basics, p. 12) at one end of each piece. Make each loop large enough so that it won't slip through the bangle's loops.

2 On one wire, string a loop on the first bangle, a pearl, and a loop on the second bangle.

3 Bend the wire to form a right angle against the second bangle's loop. Make a plain loop.

4 Repeat with the other wires, attaching pearls to every fourth loop on each bangle.

Design Guidelines

• Synthetic pearls tend to have larger holes than natural pearls. Avoid beads with small holes; fine wire will not provide enough structure for the bracelet.

• Try a monochromatic bracelet, or use a pearl strand in assorted colors, available at Rings & Things (800-366-2156, rings-things.com) or Eclectica (262-641-0910, eclecticabeads.com).

• The larger the pearl, the smaller the bracelet's inner diameter will become. Use smaller beads or coin-shaped pearls to accommodate your wrist size.

• When attaching each pearl to the bracelet, bend the wire into a right angle as close as possible to the bangle's frame. This will ensure a secure fit between the two bangles.

• For the bracelet and earrings, make 4mm or larger plain loops to accentuate the round design elements and leave ample room for the wire pieces to move.

• Create a pair of mismatched earrings with different colored pearls. Or, make one earring with two pearls and one with a single pearl.

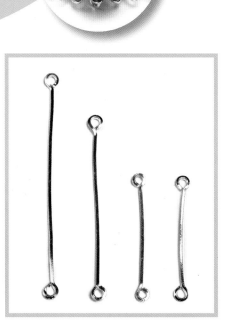
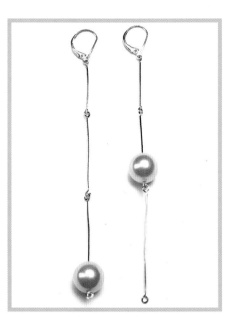

1 **earrings** • Cut six pieces of wire, two to each of the following lengths: 1¼-in., 1¾-in., and 2¼-in. (3.2cm, 4.4cm, and 5.7cm).
  Make a plain loop at one end of a 2¼-in. piece of wire. String a pearl and make a plain loop at the other end. Make a plain loop at one end of a 1¾-in. piece of wire. String a pearl and make a plain loop at the other end.

2 Make a plain loop at each end of the four remaining pieces of wire.

3 Open the loops on each 1¾-in. wire. Attach each to a short and a long wire, as shown. Close the loops. Open the loops on two earring wires and attach each dangle. Close the loops. ❖

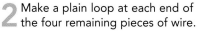

The designer offers kits for this project. See p. 255 for contact information.

Pearly girl

Cluster pearls and faceted beads on chain for a fabulous necklace, bracelet, and earrings set

by Naomi Fujimoto

The secret to this cascade of bubbly baubles? Each bead is larger than its corresponding chain link, so attaching one per link crowds and spills them playfully around your neck. For a necklace or bracelet, select a chain strong enough to support 40 or 50 beads. And don't be afraid to use dyed or synthetic beads – faux can be fabulous.

SupplyList

1 necklace • String a 12mm bead on a head pin. Make a plain loop (see Basics, p. 12) above the bead. Make a total of 35–50 dangles with various beads.

2 Determine the finished length of your necklace. (This one is 18 in./46cm.) Cut a piece of chain to that length. Open a 5mm jump ring (Basics) and attach the center dangle to the chain's center link. Close the jump ring.

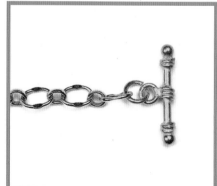

3 Open the loop on a 12mm dangle and attach it to a link next to the center dangle. Attach another 12mm dangle to the next link. Repeat on the other side of the center dangle.

4 Attach one dangle per chain link, covering approximately 6 in. (15cm) of the chain. In this necklace the pattern is: 8mm crystal, two 12mm pearls, 12mm crystal, 10mm teardrop pearl, 10mm round pearl, 8mm crystal, 12mm pearl, 8mm round pearl, 10mm crystal, 12mm pearl, 8mm crystal, 12mm pearl, 8mm round pearl, 8mm oval pearl.

5 Check the fit, allowing 1 in. (2.5cm) for the clasp. Trim an equal number of links from each end of the chain, if necessary. On each end, use a jump ring to attach half of the clasp.

1 **bracelet** • Determine the finished length of your bracelet and cut a piece of chain to that length. Make 35–50 dangles as in step 1 of the necklace. Starting at one end of the chain, attach one dangle per link until the bracelet is within 1 in. of the desired length. (Repeat the necklace pattern, omitting the jump ring unit.)

2 Check the fit, and trim chain links if necessary. Open a jump ring and attach one end of the bracelet and one end of a 1-in. chain extender. Close the jump ring. Open a dangle's loop and attach it to the end of the extender. Close the loop. Attach the other end of the bracelet and the clasp with a jump ring.

1 **earrings** • Cut a four-link piece of chain. Open the loop on an earring wire and attach the chain. Close the loop.

2 Make an 8mm, a 10mm, and a 12mm dangle as in step 1 of the necklace. Open the 10mm dangle's loop and attach it to the second chain link. Close the loop. Attach the 12mm and 8mm dangles on the third and fourth links, respectively. Make a second earring to match the first. ❖

Design Guidelines

• The largest bead size forms the majority of the beaded section in the necklace or bracelet. Change the scale by including fewer 12mm beads, or by substituting smaller beads with a delicate chain.

• Plan on 35–50 dangles to make a 6-in. (15cm) beaded section. The total number of beads is dependent on the size of the chain's links.

• For the necklace, attach the dangles in a symmetrical pattern to reduce your work in selecting and arranging beads.

• Consider substituting squares or ovals for the round beads (unusual shapes are available in limited sizes and colors).

• For a tapered effect, attach smaller beads near the ends, rather than at the center of the necklace's beaded section.

Add some sizzle to an otherwise simple strand of pearls. Create your own original pendant by wiring together rhinestone components. String a quick bracelet and earrings, and all will admire your clever take on a classic.

1 necklace • Cut a 3-in. (7.6cm) piece of silver-plated beading wire. String the wire through the four rhinestone-bridge components as shown.

A creative pendant adds pizzazz to a pearl necklace, bracelet, and earrings set

by Helene Tsigistras

bit of glitz

2 String a crimp bead on one end of the wire, and go through the crimp bead with the other end.

3 Tighten the wires and flatten the crimp bead (see Basics, p. 12). Trim the excess wire.

4 Determine the finished length of your necklace. (These are 18 in./46cm.) Add 6 in. (15cm) and cut a piece of flexible beading wire to that length.

Center the pendant on the wire. On each end, string 12mm round beads until the strand is within 1 in. (2.5cm) of the desired length.

5 On each end, string a bicone crystal, a crimp bead, a bicone, and half of the clasp. Go back through the last four beads strung and tighten the wire. Check the fit, and add or remove beads from each end if necessary. Crimp the crimp beads, and trim the excess wire.

bracelet • Determine the finished length of your bracelet, add 5 in. (13cm), and cut a piece of beading wire to that length.

String an alternating pattern of 12mm round beads and bicone crystals until the strand is within 1 in. of the desired length. End with a 12mm round.

Follow step 5 of the necklace to finish.

1 **earrings** • String a 12mm round bead and a bicone crystal on a head pin. Make a plain loop (Basics) above the top bead.

2 Open the loop on an earring wire and attach the dangle. Close the loop. Make a second earring to match the first. ❖

EDITOR'S TIPS

• Simulated pearls are available in a variety of sizes and colors. When selecting these uniformly shaped beads, look for crystal, glass, or shell pearls. Swarovski crystal pearls are sold in 24-in. (61cm) strands. That's enough to string a necklace, bracelet, and earrings.

• To make the pendant, use silver-plated beading wire. It is slightly stiffer than regular flexible beading wire, and its color matches the rhinestone-bridge components.

Supply List

necklace
- **4** 20–30mm rectangular or triangular rhinestone-bridge components (Eclectica, 262-641-0910)
- **24-in.** (61cm) strand 12mm round beads or pearls (see Editor's Tips)
- **4** 4 or 5mm bicone crystals
- **3 in.** (7.6cm) silver-plated beading wire, .018
- flexible beading wire, .014 or .015
- **3** crimp beads
- toggle clasp
- chainnose pliers
- diagonal wire cutters
- crimping pliers (optional)

bracelet
- **9–12** 12mm round beads or pearls
- **12–15** 4 or 5mm bicone crystals
- flexible beading wire, .014 or .015
- **2** crimp beads
- toggle clasp
- chainnose or crimping pliers
- diagonal wire cutters

earrings
- **2** 12mm round beads or pearls
- **2** 4 or 5mm bicone crystals
- **2** 1½-in. (3.8cm) headpins
- pair of earring wires
- chainnose pliers
- roundnose pliers
- diagonal wire cutters

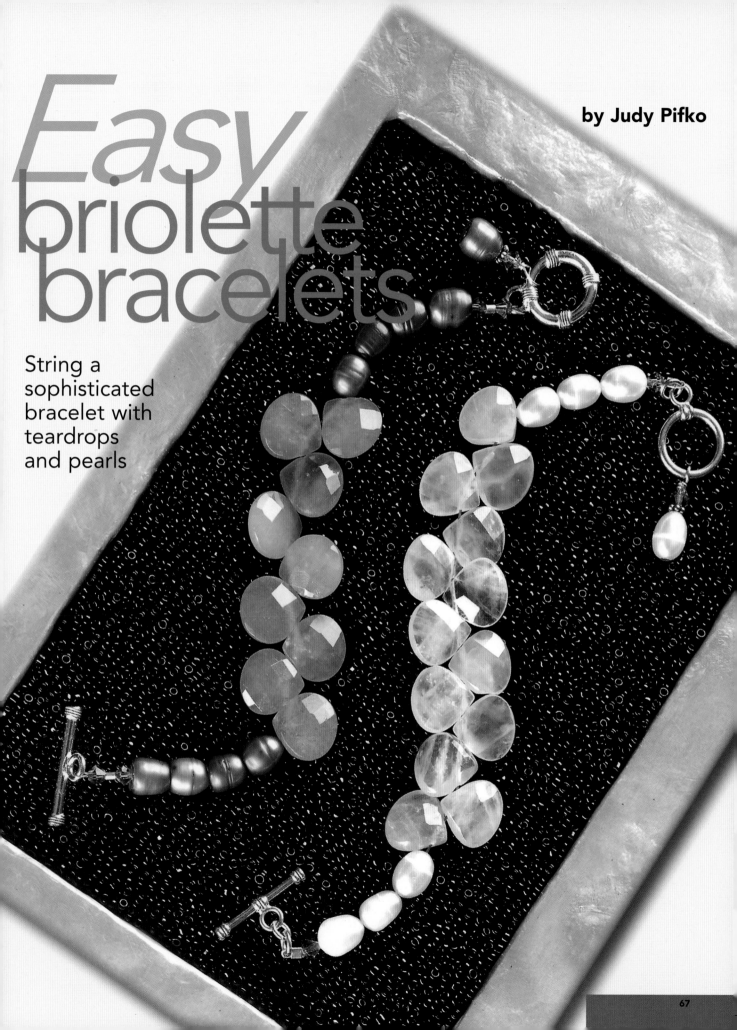

Easy briolette bracelets

by Judy Pifko

String a sophisticated bracelet with teardrops and pearls

A strand of briolettes can often be costly; this quick bracelet showcases their beauty without too much expense or effort. Alternating the position of the briolettes creates a scalloped silhouette, while teardrop pearls complement the curves. Add a pair of pearl earrings for classic, unencumbered style.

1 bracelet • Determine the finished length of your bracelet, add 5 in. (13cm), and cut a piece of beading wire to that length. String briolettes until the bracelet is half the desired length. Center the briolettes on the wire and position them in opposite directions, as shown.

2 String pearls on each end until the bracelet is within 1 in. (2.5cm) of the desired length.

3 On each end, string a crystal, a crimp bead, a crystal, and half of the clasp. Go back through the beads just strung and tighten the wires. Check the fit, and add or remove an equal number of beads from each end if necessary. Crimp the crimp beads (see Basics, p. 12), and trim the excess wire.

4 String a pearl, a flat spacer, and a crystal on a head pin. Using the largest part of your roundnose pliers, make the first half of a wrapped loop (Basics).

5 Attach the dangle's loop to the loop half of the clasp. Complete the wraps.

1 **earrings •** String a pearl, a flat spacer, a crystal, and a round spacer on a head pin. Make a wrapped loop above the spacer.

2 Open an earring wire and string the dangle. Close the wire. Make a second earring to match the first. ❖

Supply List

bracelet
- **9–13** 13mm briolettes
- **7–11** 8mm pearls
- **5 or more** 4mm bicone crystals
- 4–5mm flat spacer
- flexible beading wire, .014 or .015
- 1½-in. (3.8cm) 24-gauge head pin
- **2** crimp beads
- toggle clasp
- chainnose pliers
- roundnose pliers
- diagonal wire cutters
- crimping pliers (optional)

earrings
- **2** 8mm pearls
- **2** 4mm bicone crystals
- **2** 4–5mm flat spacers
- **2** 2mm round spacers
- **2** 1½-in. (3.8cm) 24-gauge head pins
- pair of earring wires
- chainnose pliers
- roundnose pliers
- diagonal wire cutters

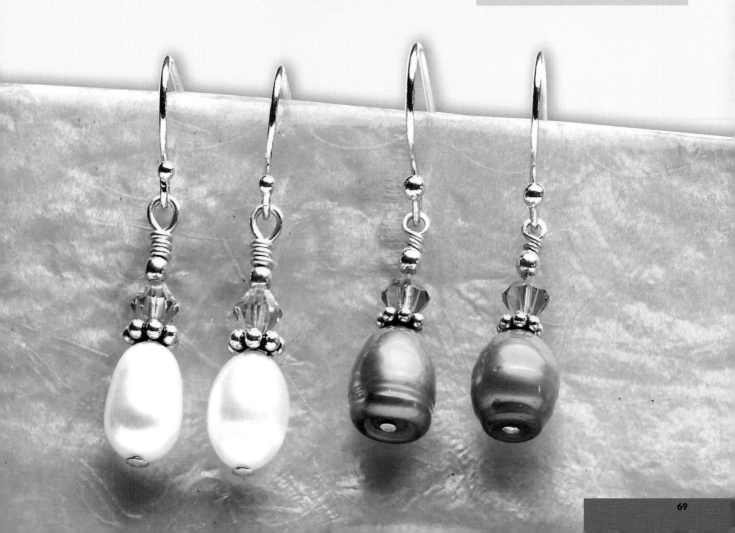

A hinged pendant opens the door to a dramatic necklace

by Rupa Balachandar

Nothing to wear for your big night out? Get in the swing with a hinged pendant. You can string this beautiful necklace quickly, and it's versatile enough to wear with any number of outfits. Choose the pendant first, and let its color be your guide as you select coordinating pearls, crystals, and rondelles. After you see how easily this fabulous necklace comes together, you'll show your wardrobe worries the door.

Swing time

1 Determine the finished length of your necklace. (These are 18 in./ 46cm.) Add 6 in. (15cm), and cut a piece of beading wire to that length. Center two to six 4mm bicone crystals on the wire. String the pendant over the bicones. String a pearl on each side.

2 On each end, string: spacer, rondelle, spacer, rondelle, spacer, bicone, spacer, rondelle, spacer, rondelle, spacer.

3 On each end, string: pearl, spacer, bicone, spacer, rondelle, spacer, bicone, spacer, pearl, spacer, bicone, spacer. String pearls until the strand is within 1 in. (2.5cm) of the desired length.

4 On each end, string: spacer, bicone, spacer, bicone, crimp bead, bicone, half of the clasp. Go back through the last beads strung and tighten the wire. Check the fit, and add or remove beads from each end if necessary. Crimp the crimp beads (see Basics, p. 12), and trim the excess wire. ❧

Supply List

- large pearl pendant
- 16-in. (41cm) strand 10mm or larger pearls
- **10** 5mm rondelles
- **16–20** 4mm bicone crystals
- **28** 5mm flat spacers
- flexible beading wire, .014 or .015
- **2** crimp beads
- toggle clasp
- chainnose or crimping pliers
- diagonal wire cutters

EDITOR'S TIP
In step 1, string enough crystals for the bail (the pendant's hanging loop) to rest on. A crystal peeking out on each side of the bail adds visual interest.

STR

You'll never lose your sense of fashion direction if you update classic pearls by twisting them with strands of stick pearls and gemstone chips. One option: Intertwine bronze pearls and aquamarine chips for an elegant combination. For a decidedly metallic direction, string steel gray chips with strands of beige and lilac pearls. Try different routes by varying the colors and sizes, and these pearly brights will keep you on course.

ANDED

Chart a fashionable course with three strands of pearls and gemstone chips • **by Betsy Baker**

1 necklace • Determine the finished length of your necklace. (These are 17 in./43cm.) Add 6 in. (15cm), and cut three pieces of beading wire to that length. On one wire, center a stick pearl. On each end, string three gemstone chips and a stick pearl, repeating until the strand is within 3 in. (7.6cm) of the desired length. Finish with gemstone chips.

2 On the second wire, string 6–9mm potato-shaped pearls until the strand is within 3 in. of the desired length.

3 On the third wire, center a 5mm potato-shaped pearl. On each end, string 1½ in. (3.8cm) of chips and a 5mm pearl, repeating until the strand is within 3 in. (7.6cm) of the desired length, and ending with chips.

4 On one end of each wire, string: six 5mm pearls, round spacer, crimp bead, spacer, half of the clasp. Go back through the last beads strung and tighten the wires. Repeat on the other end of the necklace. Check the fit, and add or remove pearls from each end if necessary. Crimp the crimp beads (see Basics, p. 12), and trim the excess wire. Alternative: String a ¼-in. (6mm) piece of bullion wire after the spacer and before the clasp on each end of the wire. Tighten the wire so the bullion forms a loop. Check the fit and add or remove beads if necessary. Crimp the crimp beads and trim the tail.

1 bracelet • Determine the finished length of your bracelet, add 5 in. (13cm), and cut three pieces of beading wire to that length. On one wire, center a stick pearl. String gemstone chips on each end until the strand is within 1 in. (2.5cm) of the desired length.

2 On the second wire, string three 6–9mm potato-shaped pearls, 1¾ in. (4.4cm) of chips, and three 6–9mm pearls. Center the beads. On each end, string chips until the strand is within 1 in. of the desired length.

3 On the third wire, center 1 in. of chips. On each end, string a 5mm potato-shaped pearl and 1 in. of chips, repeating until the strand is within 1 in. of the desired length. Follow step 4 of the necklace to finish, omitting the six 5mm pearls on each end.

1 earrings • To make a bead unit, string two 5mm potato-shaped pearls on a head pin. Make the first half of a wrapped loop (Basics) above the beads. Make a total of three bead units.

2 Cut three ½-in. (1.3cm) pieces of chain. Attach each bead unit to a chain and complete the wraps.

3 Open the loop on an earring wire. Attach each dangle and close the loop. Make a second earring to match the first. ❖

Supply**List**

necklace
- 16-in. (41cm) strand stick pearls, vertically drilled
- 16-in. (41cm) strand 6–9mm potato-shaped pearls
- 16-in. (41cm) strand 5mm potato-shaped pearls
- 36-in. (.9m) strand 5–8mm gemstone chips or keshi pearls
- **12** 3mm round spacers
- flexible beading wire, .014 or .015
- **6** crimp beads
- bullion wire (optional)
- toggle clasp
- chainnose or crimping pliers
- diagonal wire cutters

bracelet
- stick pearl, vertically drilled
- **6** 6–9mm potato-shaped pearls
- **6–8** 5mm potato-shaped pearls
- 5–8mm gemstone chips or keshi pearls, left over from necklace
- **12** 3mm round spacers
- flexible beading wire, .014 or .015
- **6** crimp beads
- bullion wire (optional)
- toggle clasp
- chainnose or crimping pliers
- diagonal wire cutters

earrings
- **12** 5mm potato-shaped pearls
- 3½ in. (8.9cm) rolo chain, 2mm links
- **6** 1½-in. (3.8cm) head pins
- pair of earring wires
- chainnose pliers
- roundnose pliers
- diagonal wire cutters

EDITOR'S TIPS
- Typically, stick pearls are available in fewer colors than potato-shaped pearls. So, select your stick pearls first, then complement them with potato-shaped pearls and gemstone chips.
- For the necklace, string the stick-pearl strand first, because its length is less adjustable than the other strands.
- String a bracelet mostly with chips, since you'll have many left over from a 26-in. (66cm) strand.
- Keep the finished diameter in mind when buying pearls and chips. If you're buying materials at a bead store, twist the three strands together to get an approximate idea of the thickness.

by Teri Bienvenue

Drape a superlong lariat over a shift or tunic for a laid-back look. Although the lariat will take a little time to string, your effort will be worth it. If you're willing to go the distance, this luminescent set will take you there in style.

Go to great lengths

1 lariat • Determine the finished length of your lariat. (The white lariat is 55 in./1.4m; the purple lariat, 58 in./1.5m.) Add 6 in. (15cm) and cut a piece of beading wire to that length. Center a spacer, a pendant, and a spacer on the wire.

2 On one side of the pendant, string: rice pearl, spacer, petal pearl, 5–10mm bead, petal, 5–10mm bead, petal, 5–10mm bead, petal.

On the other side, string a coin pearl, a rice, a spacer, and an alternating pattern of four petals and three 5–10mm beads.

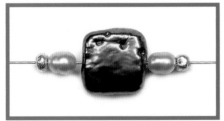

3 On each end, string: spacer, rice, coin, rice, spacer.

4 a On each end, string an alternating pattern of four petals and three 5–10mm beads. Repeat step 3.

b Repeat step 4a on one end. Repeat five times on the other end.

5 a On each end, string an alternating pattern of four petals, two 5–10mm beads, and a 12–16mm gemstone.

b On each end, repeat the pattern in step 4a until the strand is within 1 in. (2.5cm) of the desired length.

6 On each end, string: five to seven 5–10mm beads, spacer, bead tip, crimp bead, 11º seed bead. Skipping the 11º, go back through the beads just strung and tighten the wire. Check the fit, and add or remove beads if necessary. Crimp the crimp beads (see Basics, p. 12) and trim the excess wire.

7 String a 12–16mm gemstone on a head pin. Make the first half of a wrapped loop (Basics) above the bead. Attach a charm and complete the wraps.

8 Attach the dangle's loop to a bead tip's loop. Close the bead tip. Repeat steps 7 and 8 on the other end.

1 earrings • Cut a 2½-in. (6.4cm) piece of wire. Make the first half of a wrapped loop on one end. Attach a charm and complete the wraps.

2 Make a wrapped loop above the wraps.

3 String five or six beads and spacers on a head pin. Make a wrapped loop above the top bead.

4 Gently open the loop of an earring wire. Attach the bead dangle and the charm dangle. Close the loop. Make a second earring to match the first. ❧

Supply List

lariat
- 45–55mm pendant (dragonfly from Elephant Eye Beads, elephanteyebeads.com; branch from Shiana, shiana.com)
- 2 charms, approximately 15mm
- 4 12–16mm faceted gemstones
- 16-in. (41cm) strand coin pearls
- 2 16-in. (41cm) strands 6mm petal pearls
- 16-in. (41cm) strand 4mm rice pearls
- 6 16-in. (41cm) strands 5–10mm assorted beads and gemstones
- 2 11º seed beads
- 16-in. (41cm) strand 3mm spacers
- flexible beading wire, .014 or .015
- 2 2-in. (5cm) head pins
- 2 crimp beads
- 2 bead tips
- chainnose pliers
- roundnose pliers
- diagonal wire cutters
- crimping pliers (optional)

earrings
- 2 12–16mm faceted gemstones
- 2 coin pearls or other gemstones
- 2 5–10mm rondelles
- 2 charms, approximately 15mm
- 4–6 3mm spacers
- 5 in. (13cm) 26-gauge half-hard wire
- 2 2-in. (5cm) head pins
- pair of lever-back earring wires
- chainnose pliers
- roundnose pliers
- diagonal wire cutters

A necklace and earrings overflow
with a glorious array of pearls,
crystals, and gemstones

by Shannon Reeves

Get swept away by this necklace and earrings
in colors reminiscent of a day at the beach.
Patience is required when attaching these
precious bits, but like the cultivation of a
beautiful pearl, luxury is the reward.

BACK TO
NATURE

1 necklace • Cut a 3-in. (7.6cm) piece of wire. String a top-drilled pearl and make a set of wraps above it (see Basics, p. 12). Make the first half of a wrapped loop (Basics) above the wraps. Make 30–40 top-drilled units.

2 String a bead on a head pin. Make the first half of a wrapped loop above the top bead. Make 100–120 bead units. Include small beads or seed beads on some of the units.

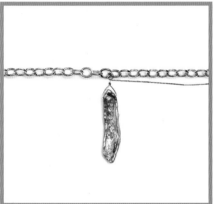

3 Determine the finished length of your necklace. (The pink necklace is 15 in./38cm; the blue necklace, 18½ in./47cm.) Cut a piece of chain to that length. Attach a top-drilled pearl unit to the center link. Complete the wraps.

4 On each side of the center unit, continue attaching bead units to the chain until the beaded section is within 6 in. (15cm) of the desired length. Attach two to four bead units per link.

5 Cut a 2½-in. (6.4cm) piece of wire. Make the first half of a wrapped loop on one end. String a 5–6mm bead and make the first half of a wrapped loop above the bead. Repeat to make a second double-loop unit.

6 Check the fit, and trim chain from each end if necessary. Keep in mind that the clasp attachment will measure about 1 in. (2.5cm). On each end, attach a double-loop unit to an end link of chain and half of the clasp. Complete the wraps.

SupplyList

necklace
- **15–19** 20–30mm stick pearls or mother-of-pearl shards, top drilled
- **15–21** 6–15mm beads, top drilled
- **100–120** 3–20mm crystals, gemstones, and pearls
- 2g 11º seed beads
- 8–11 ft. (2.4–3.4m) 24-gauge half-hard wire (for top-drilled beads)
- 16–19 in. (41–48cm) chain, 4–5mm links
- **100–120** 2-in. (5cm) 24-gauge head pins (for vertically drilled beads)
- toggle clasp
- chainnose pliers
- roundnose pliers
- diagonal wire cutters

earrings
- **2** 20–30mm stick pearls or mother-of-pearl shards, top drilled
- **2** 6–15mm beads, top drilled
- **8–14** 3–20mm crystals, gemstones, and pearls
- 6–18 in. (15–46cm) 24-gauge half-hard wire
- 1¼ in. (3.2cm) chain, 4–5mm links
- **8–14** 2-in. (5cm) 24-gauge head pins
- pair of earring wires
- chainnose pliers
- roundnose pliers
- diagonal wire cutters

1 **a earrings •** On a head pin, string one or two beads. Make the first half of a wrapped loop above the top bead.

b Cut a 3-in. piece of wire. String a top-drilled bead and make a set of wraps above it. Make the first half of a wrapped loop above the wraps. Repeat steps 1a and 1b to make six to nine bead units.

2 Cut a ½-in. (1.3cm) piece of chain. Open the loop of an earring wire and attach the chain. Close the loop. Attach the longest bead unit to the top link and complete the wraps.

3 Attach the remaining bead units to different links. Make a second earring to match the first. ✣

Weave an

Center a mother-of-pearl pendant among textured chips

This spectacular necklace looks woven, but it's far less complicated. Seed beads act as tiny anchors for the chips, giving the illusion of an intertwined rope. Suspend a mother-of-pearl pendant, then your disbelief, when you see how easily this necklace comes together.

Supply List

- mother-of-pearl pendant with bail or jump ring, approximately 40 x 60mm (Plasa Bali Beads, plasabali.com)
- 16-in. (41cm) strand mother-of-pearl or gemstone chips
- 6g 11º seed beads
- Fireline, 8-lb. test
- **2** microcrimp beads
- toggle clasp and **2** 5mm jump rings
- chainnose pliers
- roundnose pliers
- diagonal wire cutters
- microcrimping pliers (optional)

EDITOR'S TIP
Use roundnose pliers in step 2. Loop the Fireline around your pliers before going back through the chip. Remove the pliers as you tighten the line. This will ensure that the line is sufficiently taut.

1 Determine the finished length of your necklace. (These are 18 in./ 46cm.) Add 14 in. (36cm) and cut a piece of Fireline to that length. String a chip, four 11º seed beads, a pendant, and a chip. Center the beads.

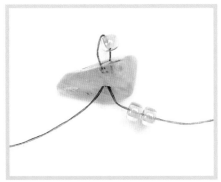

2 On each end, string a chip and an 11º. Go back through the chip and tighten the wire. String two 11ºs. Repeat until the strand is two-thirds of the desired length of the necklace.

3 On each end, string 11ºs until the necklace is within 2 in. (5cm) of the desired length. String a microcrimp bead and seven 11ºs. Go back through each crimp bead and crimp it (see Basics, p. 12). Tie an overhand knot (Basics) next to each crimp bead.

Open a jump ring (Basics). Attach half of the clasp and the seed bead loop. Close the jump ring. Repeat on the other end.

4 On each end, go back through the 11ºs strung in step 3. Tie an overhand knot. Trim the excess wire. ✤

by Yailis Feliciano

easier way

Shimmering SHELLS

by Christianne Camera

String a simple necklace, bracelet, and earrings from free-form shells

Shells are available in colors seldom seen in gemstones, such as indigo, bronze, blush, and lavender. Their substantial size makes for quick stringing – particularly when accented with crystals in coordinating hues. You'll assemble a luminescent collection in no time.

EDITOR'S TIPS
• In these projects, one 16-in. (41cm) strand of shells will make a 17-in. (43cm) necklace, a 7-in. (18cm) bracelet, and a pair of earrings. If you do not have enough beads for all three pieces, attach a chain extender to the necklace or bracelet for additional length, or make a longer necklace and skip the bracelet.
• Another option: Substitute smaller (10mm) shells for the 12–14mm shells. String two shells between each crystal.

1 **a necklace •** Determine the finished length of your necklace. (These four range from 16–19 in./41–48cm.) Add 6 in. (15cm) and cut a piece of beading wire to that length.
   b String an 11º seed bead, a crystal, an 11º, and a shell. Repeat until the necklace is within 1 in. (2.5cm) of the desired length. End with an 11º, a crystal, and an 11º.

2 On one end, string a crimp bead, an 11º, and the clasp. Go back through the last three beads strung and tighten the wire. Repeat on the other end, substituting a soldered jump ring for the clasp. Check the fit, and add or remove beads if necessary. Crimp the crimp beads (see Basics, p. 12) and trim the excess wire.

bracelet • Determine the finished length of your bracelet, add 5 in. (13cm), and cut a piece of beading wire to that length. Follow steps 1b and 2 of the necklace instructions to string the bracelet.

1 **earrings •** String a shell on a decorative head pin. Make a plain loop (Basics) above the shell.

2 Trim the head from a 1-in. (2.5cm) head pin, or cut a 1-in. piece of 24-gauge wire. Make a plain loop at one end. String a crystal and make a plain loop at the other end.

3 Open the loop on the shell unit and attach the crystal unit's loop. Close the loop. Open an earring wire and attach the dangle's top loop. Close the wire.

Make a second earring to match the first. ❖

SupplyList

necklace
- 16-in. (41cm) strand 12–14mm shell beads (Eclectica, 262-641-0910, eclecticabeads.com)
- **15–25** 4mm bicone crystals
- 1g 11º seed beads or Japanese cylinder beads
- flexible beading wire, .014 or .015
- **2** crimp beads
- lobster claw clasp and soldered jump ring
- chainnose or crimping pliers
- diagonal wire cutters

bracelet
- **7–10** 12–14mm shell beads
- **8–12** 4mm bicone crystals
- 1g 11º seed beads or Japanese cylinder beads

- flexible beading wire, .014 or .015
- **2** crimp beads
- lobster claw clasp and soldered jump ring
- chainnose or crimping pliers
- diagonal wire cutters

earrings
- **2** shell beads
- **2** 4mm bicone crystals
- **2** 1½-in. (3.8cm) decorative head pins
- **2** 1-in. (2.5cm) head pins or 2 in. (5cm) 24-gauge half-hard wire
- pair of earring wires
- chainnose pliers
- roundnose pliers
- diagonal wire cutters

Shortcuts

Readers' tips to make your beading life easier

1 cutting at an angle

During a stringing project, the ends of flexible beading wire can fray. To make finishing a breeze, trim the wire's end at an angle; the narrow tip will go back through beads more easily.
– *J. Warner, via e-mail*

2 thinking outside the box

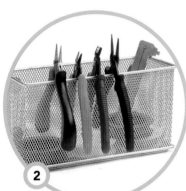

Magnetic or wire mesh containers for pens and note pads provide a compact storage area. Hang tools along one of the top edges; the inside area can hold spools of beading wire, keeping the contents visible.
– *L. Mikulsky, Green Bay, Wis.*

3 letter perfect

To organize alphabet beads, string them on a pipe cleaner (available at craft stores). Form words, or sort by letters to keep the beads easily accessible and to help you quickly see how many of a particular letter you have. Fold the ends to keep the beads in place.
– *Marie Rankin, via e-mail*

4 package deals

Many bead catalogs carry packaging and display items like small boxes, gift bags, tissue, and ribbons for purchase in bulk. Even if you don't sell your jewelry, these are handy to have on hand for gift-giving. Save money by sharing an order with a friend.
– *T. B. Scott, via e-mail*

5 security blanket

Cover your workspace with a plush Vellux blanket; beads and findings stay in one place. For a portable work area, cut an old blanket and use it to line a tray.
– *Wilma Anderson, via e-mail*

6 bridging the gap

If you see a gap between beads in a finished piece, fill the space with a crimp cover. Select a silver- or gold-colored crimp cover to match your design, then simply close the cover over the beading wire – no restringing required.
– *Elizabeth Wall, Irvington, N.J.*

Metal

and chain

Curves

by Kathie Pemberton

There's only one danger in these curves: Ease of construction can be addicting, so one bracelet may not be enough. Use either silver- or gold-plated tubes and beads of various colors — or crystals for more elegant styling. Each bracelet will take on an entirely new twist.

1 Determine the finished length of your bracelet, double that measurement, and add 5 in. (13cm). Cut a piece of beading wire to that length.

Center half of the clasp on the wire. Over both wires, string a 4mm round, a crimp bead, and a 5mm round.

Supply List

- **12 or more** 3 x 19mm curved tubes, silver- or gold-plated
- **7 or more** 8mm round beads
- **2** 5mm round beads
- **2** 4mm round beads
- flexible beading wire, .014 or .015
- **2** crimp beads
- toggle clasp or lobster claw clasp with soldered jump ring
- chainnose pliers
- diagonal wire cutters
- crimping pliers (optional)

EDITOR'S TIP
To make the bracelet longer, add 2 or 3mm round spacers at the end; to shorten, eliminate a pattern of curved tubes and use an extra 4 or 5mm round bead directly after the 8mm round bead.

2 a Leaving a small loop near the clasp, make a folded crimp (see Basics, p. 12).

b String an 8mm round over both wires. Separate the wires and string a curved tube on each strand. Repeat this pattern until the strand is within 1 in. (2.5cm) of the desired length. End with an 8mm. Check the fit, and add or remove beads if necessary.

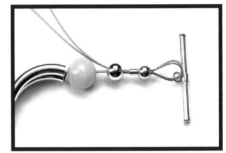

3 String a 5mm, a crimp bead, a 4mm, and the remaining half of the clasp. Go back through the last beads strung. Tighten the wires and make a folded crimp. Trim the excess wire. ❖

ahead

Combine curved tubes with beads for a supple, double-strand bracelet

Long & luscious

Create a continuous gleaming, golden necklace

by Naomi Fujimoto

Take the long view with a skinny necklace that dips down to your navel. Unfettered by a clasp, 42 inches of gold chain unite faceted lemon quartz beads. Loop the necklace around a second time for a more conservative look.

1 **necklace** • Determine the finished length of your necklace. Divide that measurement by 2.25 and cut that number of 1¾-in. (4.4cm) pieces of chain. (This necklace is 42½ in./1.1m, with a total of 19 bead units and 19 pieces of chain.) If you want a bead unit to fall in the center of the necklace, cut an odd number of chain pieces.

necklace
- **19–23** 6 x 18mm beads (faceted rectangular lemon quartz from Art Gems, artgemsinc.com)
- **38–46 in.** (1–1.2m) gold-filled half-hard 24-gauge wire
- **36–42 in.** (.9–1.1m) gold-filled cable chain, 3mm links
- chainnose pliers
- roundnose pliers
- diagonal wire cutters

earrings
- 2 6mm beads
- 2 1-in. (2.5cm) gold-filled head pins
- 5 in. (13cm) gold-filled half-hard 22-gauge wire
- 4 in. (10cm) gold-filled cable chain, 3mm links
- chainnose pliers
- roundnose pliers
- diagonal wire cutters
- metal file

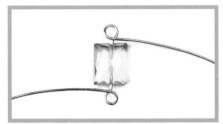

2 Cut a 2-in. (5cm) piece of wire. Make the first half of a wrapped loop (see Basics, p. 12) on one end. String a 6mm bead and make the first half of a wrapped loop on the other end. Make one bead unit for each piece of chain.

3 Attach a chain to each loop on one bead unit. Complete the wraps.

4 Continue attaching bead units and chains until the necklace is the desired length. End with a chain. Check the fit. If necessary, add or remove a bead unit or a chain, or trim an equal amount of chain from each end.

5 Attach the loop on a bead unit to each end. Complete the wraps.

1 **earrings** • **1** String a 6mm bead on a head pin and make a plain loop (Basics) above the bead. Cut a 2-in. (5cm) piece of chain. Open the loop on the bead unit and attach the chain. Close the loop.

2 Cut a 2½-in. (6.4cm) piece of wire. Bend the wire so it curves slightly. Make a plain loop at one end. Using chainnose pliers, bend the loop down so it's at a 45-degree angle from the wire.

3 Attach the chain to the loop on the wire. File the cut end of the wire, if necessary. Make a second earring to match the first. ❖

Finer things

Express your style with a retro chain necklace and earrings

by Rupa Balachandar

You can tell a lot about a gal by the way she accessorizes. The woman who wears these pieces appreciates all things vintage and is intrigued by contemporary trends. Crystal flower components dangle from an ornate filigree pendant. Shiny vermeil, a subtle contrasting detail, finishes off fine, antiqued gold chain. If you're a woman who values the finer things, try this tasteful set.

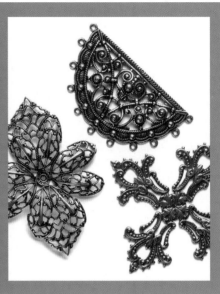

1 necklace • Determine the finished length of your necklace. (These are 25 in./64cm.) Cut a piece of chain to that length.

If the flower components have two loops, trim one off each component. File the edge if necessary.

2 Open a jump ring (see Basics, p. 12), and attach a flower component and the center leaf of the filigree pendant. Close the jump ring. Attach the remaining flower components to the filigree pendant as shown.

3 Attach a jump ring to the chain's center link. Attach another jump ring to the first jump ring and the pendant.

4 Cut a 2½-in. (6.4cm) piece of wire. Make the first half of a wrapped loop (Basics) at one end. String a 4–5mm spacer, a 4mm bicone crystal, and a spacer. Make the first half of a wrapped loop above the spacer.

5 Attach one loop to one end of the chain. Complete the wraps. Attach the other loop to a jump ring. Complete the wraps. Open a jump ring and attach a lobster claw clasp. Close the jump ring.

Repeat steps 4 and 5 on the other end, omitting the clasp.

The designer offers kits for this project. See p. 255 for contact information.

SupplyList

necklace
- 40mm or larger filigree pendant
- **3** 18mm flower components with one or two loops
- **2** 4mm bicone crystals
- **4** 4–5mm flat spacers
- 5 in. (13cm) 26-gauge half-hard wire
- 22–28 in. (56–71cm) bar-and-link chain, 3mm links
- **7** 4–5mm jump rings
- lobster claw clasp
- chainnose pliers
- roundnose pliers
- diagonal wire cutters
- metal file or emery board (optional)

earrings
- **4** 18mm flower components, with two loops
- **6** 4mm bicone crystals
- **6** 4–5mm flat spacers
- 10 in. (25cm) 26-gauge half-hard wire
- pair of earring wires
- chainnose pliers
- roundnose pliers
- diagonal wire cutters
- metal file or emery board

1 earrings • Trim the loop off one end of a flower component. File the edge if necessary. Cut a 2½-in. piece of wire. Make the first half of a wrapped loop at one end. Attach the flower component and complete the wraps.

2 String a 4–5mm spacer, a 4mm bicone crystal, and a spacer. Make the first half of a wrapped loop. Attach a two-loop flower component and complete the wraps.

3 Cut a 2½-in. piece of wire. Make the first half of a wrapped loop at one end. Attach the dangle and complete the wraps. String a crystal, a spacer, and a crystal. Make a wrapped loop perpendicular to the first loop.

4 Open the loop on an earring wire and attach the dangle. Close the loop. Make a second earring to match the first. ❖

by Naomi Fujimoto

Spacer exploration

Discover new uses for spacers in chain earrings

Spacers are often a detail in a jewelry design, rather than its foundation. Here, hammered and twisted donuts form the crux of dangly earrings – and beads are optional. Though bead possibilities seem infinite, spacers could be the final frontier for an innovative design. So, boldly go where no one has gone before with a clever pair of earrings.

EDITOR'S TIP
Attach the chain to the earring wire before attaching spacers and beads. It will be easier to pick up the earring and keep track of which link you're working on.

Supply List

- **20–40** 6–8mm donut-shaped spacers, in three styles
- 6mm rondelles (optional)
- 6 in. (15cm) cable chain, 2–3mm links
- **20–40** 4.5–5mm jump rings
- pair of earring wires
- **2** pairs of chainnose pliers, or chainnose and roundnose pliers
- diagonal wire cutters

1 Cut a 3-in. (7.6cm) piece of chain. Open the loop on an earring wire. Attach the chain, and close the loop.

2 Open a jump ring (see Basics, p. 12). Attach a spacer or rondelle to the first available link at the top of the chain. Close the jump ring.

3 Use a jump ring to attach a spacer or bead to every other link, alternating sides. Make a second earring to match the first. ❖

SHOW YOUR METAL

Connect washers and double-circle components in a modern, geometric choker

by Naomi Fujimoto

Mixed metals can be simply spectacular, especially when the components have similar shapes. This modern choker is almost retro, proving clean lines and simplicity are always in style.

1 Open a 4 x 5mm jump ring (see Basics, p. 12). Attach the 22mm washer and a hole in a solid double-circle component. Close the jump ring. Repeat on the other side, attaching an open-center double-circle component.

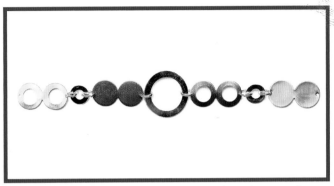

2 On each end, use a jump ring to attach a 10mm washer to the remaining hole in the double-circle component.
Use a jump ring to attach a solid or open-center double-circle component to each washer.

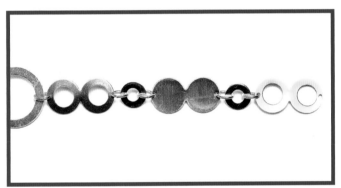

3 Repeat step 2, alternating solid and open-center components on each side, until the necklace is within 1 in. (2.5cm) of the desired length. (This necklace is 16 in./41cm.)

SupplyList

- 22mm silver washer (Metalliferous, 888-944-0909, metalliferous.com)
- **10–12** 25mm brass double-circle two-hole components, **5–6** each of solid and open-center (Metalliferous)
- **8–10** 10mm silver washers
- **20–26** 4 x 5mm oval jump rings
- toggle clasp
- **2** pairs of chainnose pliers, or chainnose and roundnose pliers

EDITOR'S TIP
In these necklaces, oval jump rings provide a more secure hold than round jump rings.

4 Use a jump ring to attach half of the clasp to each end. Check the fit, and add or remove an equal number of washers or components from each end if necessary. To lengthen the necklace only slightly, attach an extra jump ring to each end. ❖

Charming flowers
add sparkle to
this delicate set

by Tyrenia Pyskacek

Purple reign

Amethyst rules in this lightweight bracelet and earrings set that features crystal flower charms at their purple pinnacle. For a two-toned look, alternate light and dark amethyst. To get into the mixed-metal trend, assemble a pattern of crystals set in both gold and silver charms.

SupplyList

bracelet
- **12–16** 9mm crystal flower charms, **6–8** amethyst, **6–8** light amethyst (Rings & Things, rings-things.com)
- **13–17** 4mm oval jump rings
- lobster claw clasp and 5mm oval jump ring
- **2** pairs of chainnose pliers, or chainnose and roundnose pliers

earrings
- **6** 9mm crystal flower charms, **4** amethyst, **2** light amethyst
- **4** 4mm oval jump rings
- pair of earring wires
- **2** pairs of chainnose pliers, or chainnose and roundnose pliers

1 bracelet • Open a 4mm jump ring (see Basics, p. 12) and attach an amethyst flower charm and a light amethyst flower charm. Close the jump ring.

2 Alternating colors, continue to link charms with jump rings until the bracelet is within ½ in. (1.3cm) of the desired length. Attach the clasp to one end with a jump ring. Attach a 5mm jump ring to the other end.

Make a cuff-style bracelet
To make a 7-in. (18cm) cuff, you'll need 56 crystal flower charms, 106 oval jump rings, and a four-strand slide clasp.

1 Make 14 rows of four crystal charms each.

2 Connect the charms in one row to the respective charms in the next row until all rows are connected.

3 On each end, use a jump ring to attach each of the two middle flowers to their respective loops on a slide clasp. Attach two jump rings together and attach an outer flower to an outer loop of the slide clasp. Repeat with the other outer flower.

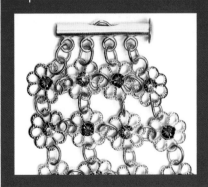

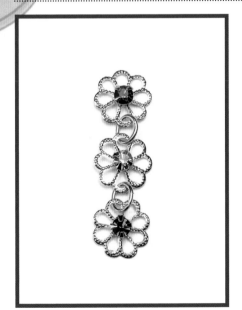

1 earrings • Open two jump rings, and attach an amethyst flower charm to each side of the light amethyst flower charm. Close the jump rings.

2 Open the loop of an earring wire and attach the dangle. Close the loop. Make a second earring to match the first. ❖

Seize the DAISIES

Embellish dangle earrings with tiny spacers

by Catherine Hodge

Daisy spacers border a briolette centerpiece, adding swing to these quick and easy earrings. Customize the dangles to your preferred length by varying the number of coils in the wire wraps.

Supply List

- **2** 5 x 8mm briolettes
- **12** 3mm daisy spacers
- 12 in. (30cm) 24-gauge half-hard wire
- pair of decorative earring wires
- chainnose pliers
- roundnose pliers
- diagonal wire cutters

1 Cut a 3-in. (7.6cm) piece of wire. String a briolette and make a set of wraps as in a top-drilled bead (see Basics, p. 12). Make a wrapped loop (Basics) above the wraps.

2 Cut a 3-in. (7.6cm) piece of wire. Center three spacers, the briolette unit, and three spacers.

3 Make a set of wraps as in a top-drilled bead. Make a wrapped loop above the wraps, perpendicular to the loop above the briolette.

4 Open the loop of an earring wire and attach the dangle. Close the loop. Make a second earring to match the first. ❖

Win a silver metal

Make a sterling silver bracelet and earrings in under 30 minutes

by Nina Cooper

String a contemporary bracelet and earrings that pair puffy disks with tiny, pale crystals. Alternate printed and matte beads; you'll love the juxtaposition of graphic patterns and smooth silver.

1 bracelet • Determine the finished length of your bracelet, add 5 in. (13cm), and cut a piece of beading wire to that length. String a printed bead, a crystal, a matte bead, and a crystal. Repeat until the bracelet is within 1 in. (2.5cm) of the desired length. End with a printed or matte bead.

2 On each end, string a spacer, a crimp bead, a spacer, and half of the clasp. Go back through the beads just strung and tighten the wire. Check the fit, and add or remove beads if necessary. Crimp the crimp beads (see Basics, p. 12) and trim the excess wire.

1 earrings • On a decorative head pin, string a crystal and a printed bead. Make the first half of a wrapped loop (Basics) above the top bead.

2 Attach the dangle to the loop of an earring wire. Complete the wraps. Make a second earring to match the first. ❖

SupplyList

bracelet
- **10–13** 13mm silver disk beads, in matte and printed styles (Nina Designs, ninadesigns.com)
- **10–13** 3mm bicone crystals
- **4** 3mm silver spacers
- flexible beading wire, .014 or .015
- **2** crimp beads
- toggle clasp
- chainnose or crimping pliers
- diagonal wire cutters

earrings
- **2** 13mm silver disk beads, in printed style (Nina Designs)
- **2** 3mm bicone crystals
- **2** 1½-in. (3.8cm) decorative head pins
- pair of earring wires (Nina Designs)
- chainnose pliers
- roundnose pliers
- diagonal wire cutters

Coin trick

Bring good fortune your way with a silver-coin necklace

by Lea Rose Nowicki

Instead of carrying a lucky penny, wear a modern necklace with five coin dangles. Whether your coins are legal tender or clever counterfeits, you'll love the fun and ease of this necklace. For an alternative design, attach gold-colored coins to a brass chain. See how far a little spare change can take you.

1 Cut a 2½-in. (6.4cm) piece of wire. Make the first half of a wrapped loop (see Basics, p. 12) at one end. String a spacer, an accent bead, and a spacer. Make the first half of a wrapped loop above the spacer. Make a total of six bead units.

2 Cut five 1–1½-in. (2.5–3.8cm) pieces of chain (see Editor's Tip), making sure each piece has a center link. Open a jump ring (Basics) and attach a coin. Close the jump ring. Open a second jump ring and attach the first jump ring and a chain's center link. Close the jump ring. Make a total of five chain units.

3 Attach a bead unit's loop to each end of a chain unit. Complete the wraps on the loops attached to the chain.

4 On each end, connect: chain unit, bead unit, chain unit, bead unit. Complete the wraps around the chain links, leaving each end loop unwrapped.

5 Determine the finished length of your necklace. (This necklace is 16 in./41cm.) Subtract the length of the coin portion of the necklace, divide that number in half, and cut two pieces of chain to that length. Attach one piece to each end loop. Complete the wraps.

6 Check the fit, and trim links from each end if necessary. Attach the clasp to one end with a jump ring. Attach a jump ring to the other end. ❖

Supply List

- 5 15–18mm coins (Fire Mountain Gems, 800-355-2137, firemountaingems.com)
- 6 6 x 8mm accent beads
- 12 4mm flat spacers
- 15 in. (38cm) 22-gauge half-hard wire
- 16–20 in. (41–51cm) chain, 4–6mm links
- 12 4mm jump rings
- lobster claw clasp
- chainnose pliers
- roundnose pliers
- diagonal wire cutters

EDITOR'S TIPS

- To make a 16-in. (41cm) or shorter necklace, cut 1-in. (2.5cm) pieces for the chain units. To make a longer necklace, use chain with larger links or cut 1½-in. (3.8cm) pieces. To simplify, use figure-eight chain or another style with long and short links, then count the number of links for each piece, rather than measuring.
- Gold-colored coins are available from All Season Trading Co., allseason.com.

All awash

Link common washers into an
uncommonly fashionable bracelet

by Lindsay Haedt

This chunky collection of rings and washers comes together in a substantial bracelet with a value beyond the sum of its parts. Washers are easy to find and easy to afford — it's the designer's eye that makes the end result anything but common.

1 a Open a 10mm jump ring (see Basics, p. 12). Attach a 6mm washer and a 5mm washer. Close the jump ring. Use a jump ring to attach the 5mm washer to another 6mm washer. Make a total of four units.

b Attach a 5mm washer to a 6mm washer with a jump ring. Attach the 6mm washer to another 5mm washer. Make a total of three units.

2 Arrange washer units in a row, alternating the two types. Begin and end with units that have a 5mm washer in the middle. Use jump rings to attach the washers in one unit to the respective washers in the next unit until all units are connected. Check the fit, allowing 3½ in. (8.9cm) for finishing. Add or remove units if necessary.

3 Use a jump ring to attach two 6mm washers. Repeat. Using three jump rings, attach each 6mm unit (including the jump ring) to the respective washers on each side.

4 Use a jump ring to attach two 5mm washers. Repeat. Attach each unit (excluding the jump ring) to the respective washers on each side. Attach a 5mm washer to each center jump ring. On each end, attach a split ring to the 5mm washer (Basics). On one end, attach a lobster claw clasp to the split ring. ✤

SupplyList

- **11–17** 6mm washers
- **13–19** 5mm washers
- **36–56** 10mm jump rings
- **2** 6–8mm split rings
- lobster claw clasp
- **2** pairs chainnose pliers, or chainnose and roundnose pliers
- split-ring pliers (optional)

EDITOR'S TIP
Washers are measured by their inside diameters. The 5 and 6mm washers have 10 and 12mm outside diameters, respectively. Find them at your local home-improvement or hardware store.

by Eva Kapitany

The Y-necklace is back, in a chain version that's more delicate than its strung predecessors. Here, gemstones decorate a gold chain, descending into a multicolored cluster pendant. Try tourmaline briolettes for an array of gorgeous greens, pinks, and browns; or, attach iolites and garnets for intense shades of blue-violet and berry. Also, incorporate smaller cubic zirconia briolettes to punctuate the necklace with sparkling bursts of color. Simple chain earrings complete the long-and-lean theme.

Brilliant

Attach
briolettes to
chain for an
updated
Y-necklace
and pretty
matching
earrings

briolettes

1 necklace • Cut a 2½-in. (6.4cm) piece of wire. String an 8 x 8mm (large) briolette and wrap as in a top-drilled bead (see Basics, p. 12). Make the first half of a wrapped loop (Basics) perpendicular to the bead. Make a total of 25–37 briolette units: 13–19 large, 12–18 small (5 x 7mm).

2 Determine the finished length of your necklace. (The purple necklace is 17½ in./44.5cm with a 2¼-in./5.7cm dangle; the green and pink necklace, 19 in./48cm with a 2½-in. dangle.) Cut two pieces of chain: one, necklace length; the other, dangle length. Attach two small-briolette units to the dangle chain's top link. Complete the wraps.

3 Attach pairs of briolette units to subsequent links, alternating small- and large-briolette units in different colors. Attach a large-briolette unit to the bottom link. Complete the wraps.

4 Open a jump ring (Basics). Attach the dangle to the necklace chain's center link. Close the jump ring. Approximately 1 in. (2.5cm) from the center, attach a large-briolette unit to a link. Complete the wraps.

5 Continue attaching briolette units at 1-in. intervals, alternating small- and large-briolette units, until the necklace is within 5 in. (13cm) of the desired length. (The necklace hangs better when there are no briolettes at the back of the neck.) Complete the wraps. Repeat on the other side.

6 Check the fit, allowing 1 in. for the clasp, and trim an equal amount of chain from each end if necessary. Use a jump ring to attach a lobster claw clasp to one end of the chain. Repeat on the other end, substituting a soldered jump ring for the clasp.

1 **earrings** • Cut a 3-in. (7.6cm) piece of chain. Fold the chain so that one side is ½ in. (1.3cm) longer than the other. Open the loop on an earring wire, and attach the folded chain's top link. Close the loop.

2 Cut a 2½-in. (6.4cm) piece of wire. String a 5 x 7mm (small) briolette and wrap as in a top-drilled bead. Make the first half of a wrapped loop. Repeat with an 8 x 8mm briolette to make a large-briolette unit,

EDITOR'S TIP
Each briolette unit calls for 2½ in. of wire. Once you make a few briolette units, note how much excess wire you trim. Then, cut each piece that much shorter. You'll use less wire and reduce the cost of the projects. The savings may not be huge here, but you'll develop good habits that prevent you from wasting wire in your future wirework projects.

3 Attach the small-briolette unit to the shorter chain. Attach the large-briolette unit to the longer chain. Complete the wraps. Make a second earring the mirror image of the first. ❧

Supply List

necklace
- **13–19** 8 x 8mm briolettes
- **12–18** 5 x 7mm briolettes
- 5–7½ ft. (1.6–2.3m) 26-gauge half-hard wire
- 19–24 in. (48–61cm) chain, 6–7mm long-and-short links
- **3** 4mm jump rings
- lobster claw clasp and soldered jump ring
- chainnose pliers
- roundnose pliers
- diagonal wire cutters

earrings
- **2** 8 x 8mm briolettes
- **2** 5 x 7mm briolettes
- 10 in. (25cm) 26-gauge half-hard wire
- 6 in. (15cm) chain, 6–7mm long-and-short links
- pair of earring wires
- chainnose pliers
- roundnose pliers
- diagonal wire cutters

Chain

Layer cable and rope chains
in a chunky necklace
and bracelet set

by Brenda Schweder

EDITOR'S TIP
Since the largest chain (13 x 21mm
links) is the least variable in length,
determine the finished length and cut
that piece first.

maker

Chainy days linger as the trend shows no signs of abating. Why not do what the forecast calls for with a project that couldn't be easier? A trio of chains in different sizes, shapes, and finishes combines with a sprinkling of spacers for an extra-long necklace or multitextured bracelet. Make one or both, and no matter how the winds of fashion blow, you'll be covered.

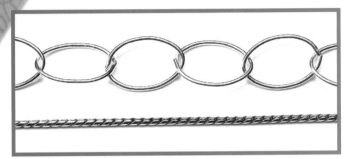

1 necklace • Determine the finished length of your necklace. (This one is approximately 24½ in./62cm.) Cut a piece of large cable chain to that length. Subtract 1 in. (2.5cm) and cut a piece of rope chain to that length.

2 Cut a piece of small cable chain 1½ in. (3.8cm) longer than the large cable chain. Center a pendant on the small cable chain.

3 Check the fit, allowing 1 in. for finishing, and trim links from each chain if necessary. Open a jump ring (see Basics, p. 12) and attach all three chains. Close the jump ring. Open another jump ring and attach the previous jump ring and half of the clasp. Close the jump ring. Repeat on the other end.

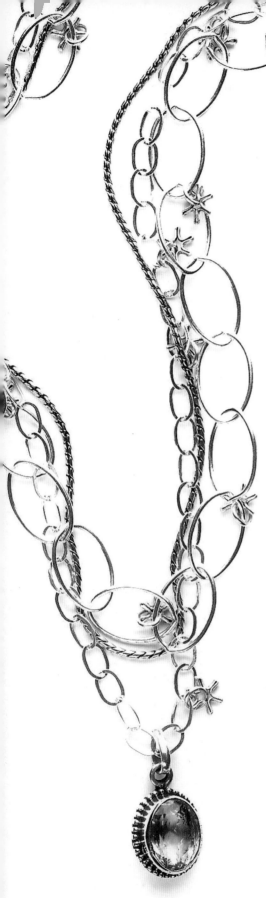

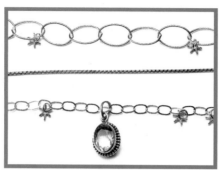

4 Use jump rings to attach spacers to the cable chains, as desired.

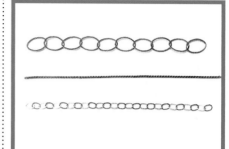

1 bracelet • Determine the finished length of your bracelet. Cut a piece of large cable chain to that length. Cut pieces of small cable and rope chain ¼–½ in. (6–13mm) longer. Attach the clasp as in step 3 of the necklace.

2 String an accent bead, a spacer, and an accent bead on a decorative head pin. Make the first half of a wrapped loop (Basics) above the top bead.

3 a Attach the dangle to the toggle half of the clasp. Complete the wraps.

b Use jump rings to attach spacers to the cable chains, as desired. ❖

The designer offers kits for these projects. See p. 255 for contact information.

SupplyList

necklace
- pendant, with bail to accommodate small cable chain
- 2–3 ft. (61–91cm) large cable chain, 13 x 21mm links (Silver City, silvercityonline.com)
- 2–3 ft. (61–91cm) small cable chain, 5 x 7mm links
- 2–3 ft. (61–91cm) rope chain, 2mm diameter
- **15–20** 8mm flat spacers (Kamol, 206-764-7375, kamolbeads@ hotmail.com)
- **19–24** 5mm jump rings
- toggle clasp
- chainnose pliers
- roundnose pliers
- diagonal wire cutters

bracelet
- 6–8 in. (15–20cm) large cable chain, 13 x 21mm links
- 6–8 in. (15–20cm) small cable chain, 5 x 7mm links
- 6–8 in. (15–20cm) rope chain, 2mm diameter
- **2** 6–10mm accent beads
- 2-in. (5cm) decorative head pin
- **7–12** 8mm flat spacers
- **11–16** 5mm jump rings
- toggle clasp
- chainnose pliers
- roundnose pliers
- diagonal wire cutters

Chain reigns

Combine a variety
of chains in an
extra-long necklace

by Rupa Balachandar

This flapper-style necklace boasts four chains in different sizes, styles, and finishes. Keep the number of beads, charms, and vintage components to a minimum, then stagger them so the chains remain the focus. Long, lean links are all the rage, so don't be surprised if you set off a chain reaction.

Supply List

- 10–12 ft. (3–3.7m) chain in four styles and finishes, 28–38 in. (71–97cm) of each
- **8–12** 12–40mm beads, vintage components, and assorted charms with hanging loops
- 10–15 in. (25–38cm) 22-gauge half-hard wire (2½ in./6.4cm per bead)
- **10–25** 4mm jump rings
- **2** 5mm jump rings
- toggle or S-hook clasp
- chainnose pliers
- roundnose pliers
- diagonal wire cutters

EDITOR'S TIP
You can have fun mixing chain styles and finishes with this project. These necklaces mix various links in silver, gunmetal, copper, and gold finishes.

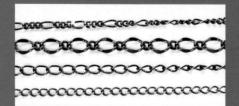

1 **a** Determine the finished length of the shortest chain of your necklace and cut a piece to that length. Cut three more pieces of chain, each 2 in. (5cm) longer than the previous one. (These chains are 30, 32, 34, and 36 in./ 76, 81, 86, and 91cm respectively.)
　b Arrange the beads and vintage components along the chains, balancing colors, finishes, shapes, and sizes.
　c To make a bead unit, cut a 2½-in. (6.4cm) piece of wire. Make a plain loop (see Basics, p. 12) at one end. String a bead on the wire and make a plain loop at the other end.

2 **a** For the chain with one bead unit, cut the chain into two equal-length pieces. Open a loop on the bead unit and attach the loop to the chain. Close the loop. Repeat on the other side of the bead unit.
　b For the chain with three bead units, cut the chain into four equal-length pieces. Attach bead units as in step 2a.

CHAIN LINKS

Here are a few Web sites that carry bulk chain in unusual finishes:

- adadornments.com
- houseofgems.com
- ornamentea.com
- rings-things.com
- rishashay.com
- tobead.com

3 **a** For the chain with three vintage components, cut the chain into four pieces. Open two jump rings and attach each end of one component to a chain. Close the jump rings. Repeat with the remaining components and pieces of chain.

 b For the chain with the charm, cut the chain into two equal-length pieces. Open a jump ring (Basics) and attach the charm's loop and each chain. Close the jump ring.

4 If necessary, trim each chain within 1 in. (2.5cm) of the desired length. Open a 5mm jump ring. Attach one end of each chain to the jump ring. Attach the 5mm jump ring to half of the clasp. Close the jump ring. Repeat on the other end. ✤

Mixed metals

Create a mixed-metal necklace with a multitude of chains

by Naomi Fujimoto

Be fearless in mixing your metals. This multistrand necklace features delicate chains in silver, gold, brass, copper, and gunmetal. For a gentle drape, use extra-fine chain in a variety of styles, such as cable, figaro, or long-and-short. You'll love the simplicity and clean lines such a combination creates.

1 Determine the finished length of your necklace. (The shortest strand of this necklace is 14¼ in./36.2cm; the longest, 22½ in./57.2cm.) Cut a piece of chain to the shortest length. Cut subsequent chains 1 in. (2.5cm) longer than the previous piece. To emphasize the top and bottom chains, cut the second and last chains 2 in. (5cm) longer than the previous piece.

2 For chains with 1.5–2mm links, open a 3mm jump ring (see Basics, p. 12) and attach it to one end of the chain. Repeat on the other end.

3 Use a 4 x 5mm oval jump ring to attach one end of each chain to half of the clasp. Check the fit, and trim the chains if necessary. (To lengthen the necklace, attach extra jump rings to each end.) Repeat on the other end with the remaining clasp half. ✤

SupplyList

- 15–26 in. (38–66cm) each of **6** or **7** kinds of chain, 1.5–4mm links
- **2–6** 4 x 5mm oval jump rings
- **2–14** 3mm jump rings (in metals to match the 1.5–2mm-link chains)
- toggle clasp
- **2** pairs of chainnose pliers, or chainnose and roundnose pliers
- diagonal or heavy-duty wire cutters

Design Guidelines

- To make a new chain look antique, add a patina with liver of sulfur or Black Max.

- For a balanced chain necklace, make the heaviest chains the longer strands.

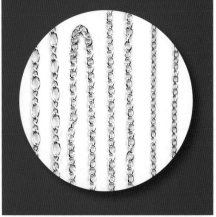

EDITOR'S TIP
Store this chain necklace on a hanger to prevent tangling. If your necklace gets tangled, open the jump ring on one side, remove the chains, untangle them, and close the jump ring.

The

by Jane Konkel

Mixed-metal earrings: yesterday's fashion faux pas, today's clever accessory

Gone are the days when fashion dictated strictly silver or head-to-toe gold. For earrings to suit your every mood, go for mixed metals. Try a pair of wavy double rings, copper crescents, or mega-hoops on for size. What once was gauche now is good, so get in the mix.

mix is in

1 **copper-crescent earrings** • To make a dangle, string a 3mm cube bead on a head pin. Make a plain loop (see Basics, p. 12) above the cube. Repeat with the remaining cubes.

2 Open a dangle's loop and attach it to the center loop of the crescent component. Close the loop. Attach the remaining dangles to every other bottom loop.

3 Cut six ½-in. (1.3cm) and two ³⁄₈-in. (1cm) pieces of chain. Open two jump rings (Basics) and attach the shorter chains to the crescent's bottom outer loops. Close the jump rings. Use jump rings to attach the longer pieces of chain to the remaining bottom loops.

4 Cut a 2-in. (5cm) piece of chain with an odd number of links. Using jump rings, attach each end to the crescent's top loops.

5 Use a jump ring to attach the center link to the loop of an earring wire. Make a second earring to match the first.

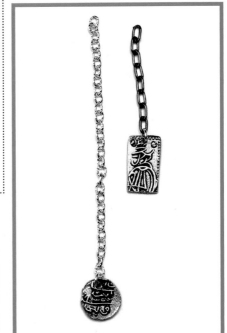

1 **hoop earrings** • Cut an 8-in. (20cm) piece of 20-gauge wire. Wrap the wire around a film canister or other round object. Remove the film canister. Cut an 8-in. piece of 4mm gunmetal chain. Pass the wire through every other link of the chain. Center the chain on the wire.

2 Cut a 2¼-in. (5.7cm) piece of silver chain and a 1-in. (2.5cm) piece of 3mm gunmetal chain.

Open a 4mm jump ring (Basics) and attach a charm to one chain. Close the jump ring. Repeat with the other charm.

3 Bend the 20-gauge wire hoop approximately 1 in. from each end to form a right angle.

Attach both chains to the horizontal wire. Wrap the horizontal wire around the vertical wire.

4 Make a wrapped loop with the vertical wire (Basics) and trim the excess.

5 Open a 5mm jump ring. Attach the dangle and the loop of an earring wire. Close the jump ring. Make a second earring to match the first.

1 double-ring earrings
Cut a 1-in. piece of gold chain. Open a gold jump ring and attach a wavy silver jump ring and the chain. Close the jump ring.

2 Cut a 1¾-in. (4.4cm) piece of silver chain. Open a silver jump ring and attach a wavy vermeil jump ring and the chain. Close the jump ring.

EDITOR'S TIP
Add a third type of metal for more visual interest. Try including gunmetal with the crescent pair, brushed silver with the hoops, or antiqued or oxidized metal with the double-ring pair.

3 Open a silver jump ring and attach both chains and the loop of an earring post. Close the jump ring.

To make a second earring, cut a 1-in. piece of silver chain and attach a wavy vermeil jump ring. Cut a 1¾-in. (4.4cm) piece of gold chain and attach a wavy silver jump ring. Repeat step 3. ❖

Grab the brass ring

by Brenda Schweder

Mix assorted chains
with a round focal piece
for a prize bracelet

You keep your eyes on the prize, so why shouldn't your jewelry reflect that? An etched free-form circle, or even a vintage belt ring, makes a great focal piece for a mixed-chain bracelet. The best part is, you don't have to worry about matching all your findings. Dare to pair a silver jump ring with a brass clasp, or incorporate old metals with new for a winning combination.

1 Open a 7–10mm jump ring (see Basics, p. 12). String an end link of each of the six chains. Wrap the chains around the focal component and string a link of each chain on the jump ring. Close the jump ring and trim the excess chain.

2 Use a 5mm jump ring to attach metal charms to the 7–10mm jump ring.

3 Determine the finished length of your bracelet, subtract the diameter of the focal component, and divide that number in half. Cut two pieces of each chain to that length. Use a 5mm jump ring to attach one set of chains to the 7–10mm jump ring. Set aside the other set of chains.

Supply List

- 30–40mm round focal component (donut: Rings & Things, rings-things.com; circle: from Brenda Schweder, brendaschweder.com)
- **2–3** 12–25mm metal charms
- 10mm large-hole metal accent bead
- 7–10 in. (18–25cm) each of **6** kinds of chain in different styles and finishes, 3–9mm links
- 10–12mm 14- or 16-gauge jump ring, to accommodate the thickness of the focal component (optional)
- 7–10mm 16- or 18-gauge jump ring
- **4–6** 5mm 18-gauge jump rings
- clasp
- **2** pairs of chainnose pliers, or chainnose and roundnose pliers
- diagonal or heavy-duty wire cutters

4 Open a 10–12mm jump ring. Attach the remaining set of chains and the focal component. If the component has an attached loop, use a 5mm jump ring to attach the chains to the loop. String a large-hole metal accent bead on the finest chain.

5 Use a 5mm jump ring to attach the working end of each set of chains to half of the clasp. Check the fit, and trim the chains or attach an additional jump ring if necessary. ✤

EDITOR'S TIP
When wrapping chain around the focal component, close the jump ring before trimming the excess chain. This is easier than trying to connect short pieces of chain with a jump ring.

The designer offers kits for this project. See p. 255 for contact information.

String a featherweight choker with colorful mesh ribbon

by Stacey Neilson

Mesh

Isn't it time to lighten up? The mesh in this choker looks and feels as light and airy as ribbon. You'll enjoy stretching, twisting, and knotting it into intriguing shapes. Aside from its undulating lines and flourish of colors, this choker's finest feature is that it can be strung in a matter of minutes.

SupplyList

- **12** 6º seed beads
- **6** 4-ft. (1.2m) pieces WireLace ribbon in four colors (Mimi's Gems, 714-377-8666, mimisgems.com)
- three-strand clasp

1 String two 4-ft. (1.2m) pieces of mesh ribbon through each loop of one half of the clasp, centering the clasp on the ribbons.

2 String one end of each pair of ribbons through the respective loop of the other half of the clasp. Adjust one ribbon from each pair so the dangling ribbons are of unequal lengths. Check the fit, and tie a surgeon's knot (see Basics, p. 12) in each pair approximately ¼ in. (6mm) from the clasp.

3 String a 6º seed bead on one end of a ribbon. Tie an overhand knot (Basics) below the seed bead, and trim the excess ribbon. Repeat with the remaining ribbon ends.

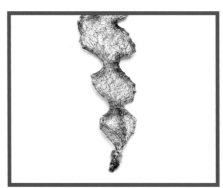

4 To get a rippled effect gently pull apart the sides of one ribbon at the desired intervals, leaving the upper third of the ribbon intact. Repeat with each remaining ribbon. ❖

around

EDITOR'S TIP
If it is difficult to pass the mesh ribbon through the clasp's loop, make a loop with a piece of flexible beading wire and string the ribbon through the loop. String both ends of the beading wire through the clasp's loop, and the mesh ribbon will follow.

Metal
morphosis

Transform wire into a ring in a matter of minutes • **by Sara Strauss**

Use deep, rich colors or bold brights as you incorporate different beads into your ring design. This project is easy and addictive, so go ahead and make many – you'll have a ring for any season.

Supply List

- 3 3–10mm beads
- 3½ in. (8.9cm) 18- or 20-gauge dead-soft wire
- 6 in. (15cm) 24- or 26-gauge half-hard wire
- chainnose pliers
- roundnose pliers
- bentnose pliers (optional)
- diagonal wire cutters
- ring mandrel

EDITOR'S TIP
For a thicker band, start with an 8-in. (20cm) piece of 18- or 20-gauge wire and wrap it several times around the ring mandrel. Use a 10-in. (25cm) piece of 24- or 26-gauge wire to attach the beads.

1 Locate your ring size on a ring mandrel and wrap a 3½-in. (8.9cm) piece of 18- or 20-gauge wire snugly around the mandrel.

2 Remove the wire from the mandrel and make a loop at one end.

3 Make a small half-loop at the end of a 6-in. (15cm) piece of 24- or 26-gauge wire and attach it to the ring, as shown.

4 Using either chainnose or bentnose pliers, hold the band in place. Make three or more wraps around the ring with the 24- or 26-gauge wire.

5 String a bead and make three or more wraps around the ring. Repeat two more times.

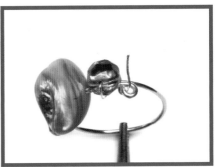

6 Pass the wire up through the ring's loop.

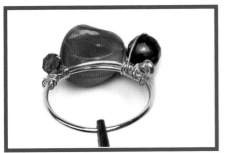

7 Tuck the end of the wire under one of the beads. Trim the excess wire. ✤

Twist a
dainty display
of gemstones or
pearls, and expand
your wirework
repertoire

by Jill Italiano

Branch out

This delicate collar of branches flecked with tiny gemstones looks complicated, but isn't. Once you shape the first branch unit, it won't take long to make and connect the remaining ones. Proportional hoop earrings are simple accents that keep the focus rooted in the necklace.

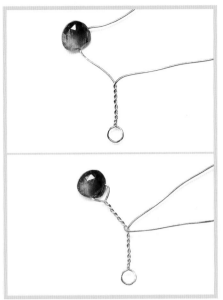

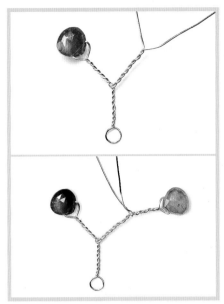

1 necklace • Cut a 12-in. (30cm) piece of wire. Using roundnose pliers, make a loop in the center of the wire. Twist the wires together, making a ⅜-in. (1cm) stem.

2 a Separate the wires. On one wire, string a top-drilled bead ½ in. (1.3cm) from the end of the stem.

b Twist the wires together to form a branch, stopping when you reach the stem.

3 a Twist the wires together to form a ⅜-in. branch.

b On the longer wire, string a bead ½ in. from the branch just made. Bring the longer wire around the bead and twist the wires together to form a branch.

EDITOR'S TIP

In steps 2 and 3 of the necklace, remember to string the second and third beads of each unit on the longer wire. This will ensure that enough wire remains for the wrapped loop.

4 Twist the wires together to form a ½-in. branch. On the longer wire, string a bead ⅜ in. from the branch just made. Form a branch.

5 Twist the wires together to form a ⅜-in. branch. Make the first half of a wrapped loop (see Basics, p. 12).

Turn the stem loop perpendicular to the branches. Using roundnose pliers, curve the branches. Make 10 to 12 units. (These necklaces are 15 in./38cm; each has ten units.)

SupplyList

necklace
- **31–37** 4–5mm beads, top drilled
- 10½–12½ ft. (3.2–3.8m) 26-gauge dead-soft wire
- **2** 3–4mm jump rings
- lobster claw clasp
- 2 in. (5cm) chain for extender, 4–5mm links
- chainnose pliers
- roundnose pliers
- diagonal wire cutters

earrings
- **2** 4–5mm beads, top drilled
- 7 in. (18cm) 20-gauge half-hard wire
- 5 in. (13cm) 26-gauge dead-soft wire
- chainnose pliers
- roundnose pliers
- diagonal wire cutters
- ball-peen hammer
- bench block or anvil
- metal file or emery board

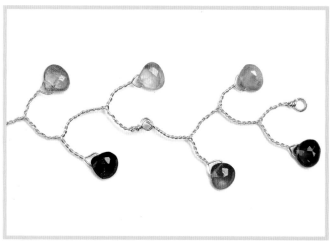

6 Attach one unit's first half of a wrapped loop to the stem loop of another unit. Complete the wraps. Attach units, flipping every other unit, until the necklace is within 1 in. (2.5cm) of the desired length. Complete the wraps on the end loops.

7 Cut a 2-in. (5cm) piece of wire and center a bead on it. Twist the wires together to make a ¼-in. (6mm) stem above the bead. Make the first half of a wrapped loop above the stem.

Cut a 2-in. piece of chain for an extender. Attach the loop to the end link of chain and complete the wraps.

8 Open a jump ring (Basics). On one end, attach the end unit's loop and a lobster claw clasp. Close the jump ring. Repeat on the other end, substituting the chain extender for the clasp.

1 earrings • Cut a 2½-in. (6.4cm) piece of 26-gauge wire. String a top-drilled bead and make a set of wraps above it (Basics). Make a wrapped loop above the wraps.

3 Hammer the hoop on a bench block or anvil, avoiding the loop and bent end. Turn the hoop over and hammer the other side.

String the bead unit. Make a second earring to match the first. ❖

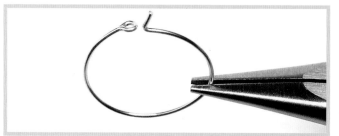

2 Cut a 3½-in. (8.9cm) piece of 20-gauge wire. Wrap the wire around a wide-tip marker barrel or other round object. Make a plain loop (Basics) on one end of the wire. Bend the other end up to form a right angle. Trim the excess wire to ⅛ in. (3mm) and file the end.

Shortcuts

Readers' tips to make your beading life easier

1 hammer time

Hardening head pins or findings usually requires a bench block or anvil. In a pinch, substitute a large hammer turned on its side. The hammer's head provides a hard, flat surface for pounding the wire.
– *Pam Pollard, Coweta, Okla.*

2 muffin tins

Use a muffin tin to sort beads. With a dozen cups, a tin is perfect for projects that require many different beads. To make cleanup easier, put paper liners in the tins first, then simply pour the beads back into their containers.
– *C. C. Lilly, via e-mail*

3 plain-loop perfection

To make plain loops, put your finger against the head pin underneath the bead. You'll be able to bend the head pin closer to the bead, so your loop will show less excess wire.
– *Sarah Keefe, Boston, Mass.*

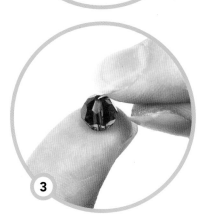

4 jewelry hangups

A belt hanger with hooks is a handy way to store jewelry. The holder organizes 12 or more necklaces while occupying minimal space in your closet, and your jewelry is less likely to get tangled.
– *E. Jones, via e-mail*

5 flexible finishing

To build flexibility into a strung bracelet's length, string a crimp bead onto a jump ring. String a crimp bead and spacer on the end of the strand. Thread the wire through the jump ring's crimp bead, go back through the last beads strung, and crimp the bracelet's crimp bead. Attach the clasp with a jump ring. Adjust the length by adding extra jump rings to the first one without restringing.
– *Marie Rankin, via e-mail*

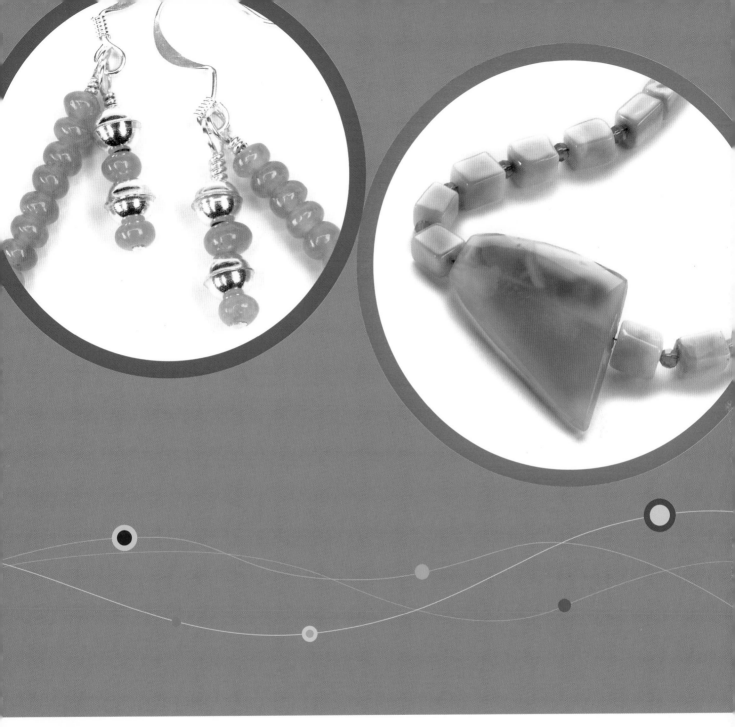

Gemstones

An old accoutrement
takes on new life in a gemstone
necklace

by Rupa Balachandar

Pinned on lapels, sweaters, purses, and even at the waist, brooches remain firmly attached to the fashion scene. Just when you thought it's all been done, there's yet another place for that pin – a necklace. Coordinate nuggets or tube beads in color and proportion with your brooch. Pin it a bit off center, and you'll have a fresh and stylish accessory. Leftover beads strung on wire make for a quick pair of stylish hoops.

New spin
for a pin

1 necklace • Determine the finished length of your necklace. (This one is 16 in./ 41cm.) Add 6 in. (15cm) and cut a piece of beading wire to that length. String a nugget or a tube bead, a spacer, a gemstone chip, and a spacer. Repeat this pattern until the necklace is within 2 in. (5cm) of the desired length. End with a nugget or a tube bead.

2 On each end, string: spacer, 3mm round, crimp bead, 3mm round, jump ring. Go back through the last beads strung and tighten the wires. Check the fit, and add or remove beads if necessary. Crimp the crimp beads (see Basics, p. 12), and trim the excess wire.

   Attach the S-hook clasp to each jump ring. Close one side of the hook with chainnose pliers if desired.

3 Pin the brooch over the wire between two beads.

Supply List

necklace
• brooch (silver brooch from Rupa Balachandar, rupab.com)
• 16-in. (41cm) strand 15–20mm gemstone nuggets or 8–10mm tube beads
• **20–30** 3–5mm gemstone chips
• **32–42** 4–5mm flat or heishi spacer beads
• flexible beading wire, .014 or .015 for tube beads, .018 or .019 for nuggets
• **4** 3mm round beads
• **2** 5mm jump rings
• **2** crimp beads
• hook-and-eye or S-hook clasp
• chainnose or crimping pliers
• diagonal wire cutters

earrings
• **2** 8–10mm tube beads
• **4** 3–5mm gemstone chips
• **8** 4–5mm flat or heishi spacer beads
• 12 in. (30cm) 24-gauge half-hard wire
• pair of earring wires
• chainnose pliers
• roundnose pliers
• diagonal wire cutters

1 **earrings** • Cut a 6-in. (15cm) piece of 24-gauge wire. Center a tube bead on the wire. On each side of the tube bead, string a spacer, a gemstone chip, and a spacer.

2 Bring each wire end up to make a teardrop shape. Starting ¾ in. (2cm) from each end, bend the wires to form a right angle. Wrap the horizontal wire around the vertical wire three times and trim the excess wrapping wire. Make a wrapped loop (Basics) with the remaining wire.

3 Open an earring wire. Attach the dangle and close the wire. Make a second earring to match the first. ❖

Golden opportunity

Pair gemstone nuggets with gold
accents for a quick necklace,
bracelet, and earrings set

by Betsy Baker

A classic choker looks contemporary when strung with irregularly shaped gemstone nuggets. Any gemstone with golden highlights will dazzle: Try shells, turquoise, citrine, carnelian, or stick pearls. Sprinkled with vermeil accents in smooth and textured finishes, the necklace's sophisticated style belies its simple stringing. And since the necklace is choker length, you'll get extra mileage from a 16-inch strand of nuggets – enough for a choker, a bracelet, and a pair of earrings.

1 **a necklace** • Determine the finished length of your necklace. (These are 15½ in./39.4cm.) Add 6 in. (15cm) and cut a piece of beading wire to that length.
b Center a nugget on the wire. On each end, string a textured vermeil bead and a nugget, repeating until the necklace is half the desired length. End with a vermeil bead.

2 String a nugget and a vermeil spacer on each end, repeating until the necklace is within 2½ in. (6.4cm) of the desired length. String two 6mm round beads on each end.

3 On each end, string a round spacer, a crimp bead, a round spacer, and a soldered jump ring. Go back through the beads just strung and tighten the wire. Check the fit, and add or remove beads if necessary. (If desired, check the fit, then string a ¼-in./6mm piece of bullion between the spacer and the jump ring. Tighten the wire so the bullion forms a loop.) Crimp the crimp beads (see Basics, p. 12) and trim the excess wire.

4 Attach an S-hook clasp to one of the jump rings. Close half of the S-hook with chainnose pliers.

EDITOR'S TIP
For a more traditional necklace, select geometric shapes such as rectangles, ovals, or rounds.

bracelet • Determine the finished length of your bracelet, add 5 in. (13cm), and cut a piece of beading wire to that length. Follow steps 1b and 2 of the necklace instructions. To finish, follow step 3, substituting a lobster claw clasp for one of the soldered jump rings.

1 **earrings** • String a nugget and a round or vermeil bead on a head pin. Make a wrapped loop (Basics) above the top bead.

2 Open the loop on a post earring and attach the dangle. Close the loop. Make a second earring to match the first. ✤

Supply List

necklace
- 16-in. (41cm) strand gemstone nuggets, approximately 15 x 18mm
- **6–10** 5–7mm textured vermeil beads
- **8–12** 5mm vermeil spacers
- **4** 6mm round beads
- **4** 3mm round spacers
- flexible beading wire, .014 or .015
- **2** crimp beads
- bullion wire (optional)
- S-hook or hook clasp with **2** soldered jump rings
- chainnose pliers
- diagonal wire cutters
- crimping pliers (optional)

bracelet
- **5–7** gemstone nuggets, approximately 15 x 18mm
- **2–4** 5–7mm textured vermeil beads
- **4** 5mm vermeil spacers
- **4** 6mm round beads
- **4** 3mm round spacers
- flexible beading wire, .014 or .015
- **2** crimp beads
- bullion wire (optional)
- lobster claw clasp and soldered jump ring
- chainnose or crimping pliers
- diagonal wire cutters

earrings
- **2** gemstone nuggets, approximately 15 x 18mm
- **2** 5–7mm textured vermeil beads or 6mm round beads
- **2** 2-in. (5cm) head pins
- pair of post earrings with loops
- chainnose pliers
- roundnose pliers
- diagonal wire cutters

Make a bold
statement with
this distinctive
accented bracelet

by Irina Miech

All in

Capitalize on fundamental design elements to create this sumptuous bracelet. Although this piece speaks opulence, it's refreshingly easy and affordable. Ornate bead caps crown each faceted bead and are available in economical base metal. Captivating and cost-effective, this bracelet will give you quick returns on your investment.

1 Determine the finished length of your bracelet. Add 5 in. (13cm), and cut a piece of beading wire to that length. Center an 11º seed bead, a rectangular bead cap, a rectangle bead, a rectangular bead cap, and an 11º on the wire.

2 On each end, string: round bead cap, rondelle or round bead, round bead cap, 11º, rectangular bead cap, rectangle bead, rectangular bead cap, 11º. Repeat until the strand is within 1 in. (2.5cm) of the desired length. End with a bead cap.

3 On each end, string an 11º, a crimp bead, an 11º, and half of the clasp. Go back through the last beads strung and tighten the wire. Check the fit, and add or remove beads from each end if necessary. Crimp the crimp beads (see Basics, p. 12), and trim the excess wire. ❖

Supply List

- **5–7** 10 x 12mm faceted rectangles
- **6–8** 9mm faceted rondelles or round beads
- **10–14** 9mm rectangular bead caps (Eclectica, 262-641-0910)
- **12–16** 7–9mm round bead caps (Eclectica)
- 1g 11º seed beads
- flexible beading wire, .014 or .015
- **2** crimp beads
- toggle clasp
- chainnose or crimping pliers
- diagonal wire cutters

The designer offers kits for this project. See p. 255 for contact information.

EDITOR'S TIP
It's not necessary to limit yourself to just one or two colors. Experiment with various color schemes for a truly unique bracelet.

caps

Multifaceted

Rich hues of gemstones and pearls combine in a striking necklace, bracelet, and earrings set • **by Jennifer Seneca**

Elevate a simple strung necklace to the next level by mixing pearls and faceted nuggets with a framework of spacers and bead caps. Start with a brightly colored gemstone, such as dyed green agate, or go the natural route with an earthy Botswana agate. Don't skimp on the details; choose unique bead caps and an ornate box clasp. You may spend a little more time searching for materials, but the results will be stunning: professional-quality jewelry that suits a variety of styles.

1 **a necklace** • Determine the finished length of your necklace. (These are 17½ in./44.5cm.) Add 6 in. (15cm) and cut a piece of beading wire to that length.

b String: two 4mm spacers, 3mm spacer, 4mm spacer, 6mm spacer, nugget, 6mm spacer, 4mm spacer, 3mm spacer, two 4mm spacers. Center the beads on the wire.

2 On each end, string: three pearls, two 4mm spacers, bead cap, round gemstone, bead cap, two 4mm spacers, three pearls. Repeat the patterns in steps 1b and 2 on each end.

magic

3 On each end, string: two 4mm spacers, bead cap, round gemstone, bead cap, two 4mm spacers, pearl. Repeat until the necklace is within 1 in. (2.5cm) of the desired length.

4 On each end, string: two 4mm spacers, 3mm spacer, crimp bead, 3mm spacer, half of the clasp. Go back through the beads just strung and tighten the wire. Check the fit, and add or remove beads from each end if necessary. Crimp the crimp beads (see Basics, p. 12), and trim the excess wire.

1 a **bracelet** • Determine the finished length of your bracelet, add 5 in. (13cm), and cut a piece of beading wire to that length. String the pattern in step 1b of the necklace. Center the beads on the wire.

b On each end, string: pearl, two 4mm spacers, bead cap, round gemstone, bead cap, two 4mm spacers. Repeat until the bracelet is within 1 in. (2.5cm) of the desired length.

SupplyList

necklace
- **3** 23 x 28mm faceted gemstone nuggets
- 16-in. (41cm) strand 6–8mm potato-shaped pearls
- **6–10** 10–12mm round gemstones
- **6** 6mm flat spacers
- **40–60** 4mm flat spacers
- **10** 3mm round spacers
- **12–20** bead caps
- flexible beading wire, .014 or .015
- **2** crimp beads
- box clasp
- chainnose or crimping pliers
- diagonal wire cutters

bracelet
- 23 x 28mm faceted gemstone nugget
- **5–7** 6–8mm potato-shaped pearls
- **4** 10–12mm round gemstones

- **2** 6mm flat spacers
- **26–34** 4mm flat spacers
- **6** 3mm round spacers
- **8** bead caps
- flexible beading wire, .014 or .015
- 1½-in. (3.8cm) head pin
- **2** crimp beads
- lobster claw clasp
- 1½ in. (3.8cm) chain for extender
- chainnose or crimping pliers
- diagonal wire cutters

earrings
- **2** 10–12mm round gemstones
- **2** 6–8mm potato-shaped pearls
- **6** 4mm flat spacers
- **2** 3mm round spacers
- **4** bead caps
- **2** 2-in. (5cm) head pins
- pair of earring wires
- chainnose pliers
- roundnose pliers
- diagonal wire cutters

2 On one end, string a 3mm spacer, a crimp bead, a 3mm spacer, and a 1½-in. (3.8cm) piece of chain. Go back through the beads just strung and tighten the wire. Repeat on the other end, substituting a lobster claw clasp for the chain. Check the fit, and add or remove beads from each end if necessary. Crimp the crimp beads, and trim the excess wire.

3 To make the extender's dangle, string two 4mm spacers, a pearl, and two 4mm spacers on a head pin. Make the first half of a wrapped loop (Basics) above the spacers, and attach the loop to the chain's end link. Complete the wraps. ❖

1 **earrings** • On a head pin, string: 4mm spacer, pearl, 4mm spacer, bead cap, round gemstone, bead cap, 4mm spacer, 3mm spacer. Make a wrapped loop (Basics).

2 Open the loop on an earring wire and attach the dangle. Close the loop. Make a second earring to match the first.

A sprinkling of interesting beads creates a quick visual treat

Feast for the eyes

The donut may be the centerpiece of this necklace, but your creativity is the main ingredient. Accent the focal bead with sprinkles of color to suit your taste. Whip up some instant hoop earrings to round out the look.

1 necklace • Determine the finished length of your necklace. (These are 14½ in./36.8cm.) Add 10 in. (25cm) and cut a piece of beading wire to that length.

Center 5 in. (13cm) of 11º seed beads on the wire and string both ends through an accent bead, creating a loop.

2 Separate the wires. On each end, string three 11ºs and a pattern of beads and spacers until the necklace is within 1 in. (2.5cm) of the desired length.

3 On each end, string a 5mm round spacer, a crimp bead, and half of the clasp. Go back through the beads just strung and tighten the wire. Check the fit, and add or remove beads from each end if necessary. Crimp the crimp beads (see Basics, p. 12), and trim the excess wire.

by Denise Baum

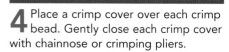

4 Place a crimp cover over each crimp bead. Gently close each crimp cover with chainnose or crimping pliers.

5 Slide the seed bead loop through the donut's hole. Bring both ends of the necklace through the loop and tighten.

1 earrings • String a 1-in. (2.5cm) pattern of beads and spacers as desired on a hoop earring.

2 Using chainnose pliers, bend the wire up ⅛ in. (3mm) from the end. Make a second earring to match the first. ❖

EDITOR'S TIP
No one can have just one donut. Create different looks by changing the removable pendant to one of a different color or material.

Supply List

necklace
- 50mm donut
- 18–24mm accent bead
- **8–10** 10–12mm nuggets
- **2–4** 8–10mm round beads
- **4–6** 6–12mm rondelles
- **8–10** 6–8mm crystals
- **20–24** 4mm round beads
- 2g 11º seed beads
- **24–28** 4–8mm flat silver spacers

- **2** 5mm round silver spacers
- flexible beading wire, .014 or .015
- **2** crimp beads
- **2** crimp covers
- toggle clasp
- chainnose pliers
- diagonal wire cutters
- crimping pliers (optional)

earrings
- **10–18** 4–12mm beads and spacers
- 1-in. (2.5cm) pair of hoop earrings
- chainnose pliers

Half & half

String an atypical pattern in a three-strand necklace

by **Shruti Gautam Dev**

Throw convention off balance with an asymmetrical necklace.
The two halves – geometric shapes and free-form chips – meet at
off-kilter nuggets. For a unifying element, add earrings with a clean,
simple line. You'll love the dramatic drape of these pieces.

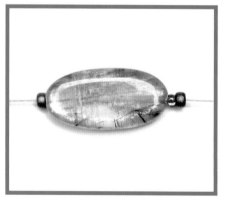

1 **necklace** • Determine the finished length of your necklace. (The shortest strand of these is 15½ in./39.4cm.) Add 6 in. (15cm) and cut a piece of beading wire to that length. Cut two more pieces, each 3 in. (7.6cm) longer than the previous piece. On each wire, center an 8º seed bead or 2mm bead, a nugget, an 11º seed bead, and an 8º.

2 On one end of the shortest wire, string a flat bead, an 8º, an 11º, and an 8º. Repeat five times. String a flat bead and an 8º.

3 On the other end of the shortest wire, string three heishi beads or chips and an 8º. Repeat ten times.

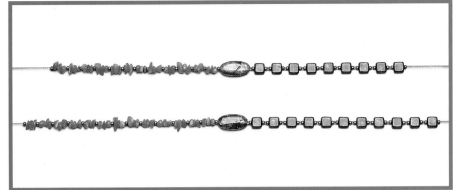

4 On one end of the middle wire, string the pattern in step 2 eight times. String a flat bead and an 8º. On the other end, string the pattern in step 3, and repeat 11 times.

5 On one end of the longest wire, string the pattern in step 2 ten times. String a flat bead and an 8º. On the other end, string the pattern in step 3, and repeat 12 times.

6 On each end of each strand, string an 8º and a 3–4mm bead. Repeat until each strand is within 1 in. (2.5cm) of the desired length. End with a 3mm bead.

7 Arrange the strands so the nuggets are staggered with the middle strand's nugget in the center. Check the fit, and add or remove beads from each end if necessary. Allow 1 in. for finishing.

8 On each end, string an 11º, a crimp bead, an 11º, and the corresponding loop of half of the clasp. Go back through the beads just strung and tighten the wires. Crimp the crimp beads (see Basics, p. 12), and trim the excess wire.

Supply List

necklace
- **3** nuggets, approximately 15 x 25mm
- **27** 8mm flat beads
- 16-in. (41cm) strand 5mm heishi beads or chips
- **73–130** 3–4mm beads
- 3g 8º seed beads or 16-in. (41cm) strand 2mm beads
- 2g 11º seed beads
- flexible beading wire, .014 or .015
- **6** crimp beads
- three-strand clasp
- chainnose or crimping pliers
- diagonal wire cutters

earrings
- **2** 8mm flat beads
- **2** 5mm heishi beads or chips
- **2** 8º seed beads or 2mm beads
- **2** 1½-in. (3.8cm) head pins
- pair of earring wires
- chainnose pliers
- roundnose pliers
- diagonal wire cutters

SUPPLY NOTES

Materials for the turquoise necklace are available from Rings & Things, (800) 366-2156, or rings-things.com. Materials for the Czech glass and chrysoprase set are available from Knot Just Beads, (414) 771-8360, or orders@knotjustbeads.com.

1 earrings • On a head pin, string a flat bead, a heishi bead or chip, and an 8º seed bead. Make a plain loop (Basics) above the bead.

2 Open the loop of an earring wire. Attach the dangle and close the loop. Make a second earring to match the first. ✤

Get back to black with a triple-strand necklace and glamorous earrings

Just as the fashion forecasters predicted, black is back. But unlike gothic accessories, today's jet gems are all glam. Combine three different strands, incorporating assorted shapes and textures, to take your outfit from simple to spectacular. Add onyx earrings, and you may find that turning to the dark side has its rewards.

1 necklace • Determine the finished length of the short strand of your necklace. (The short strand on this necklace is 16 in./41cm.) Add 6 in. (15cm) and cut a piece of beading wire to that length. Center a 6º seed bead, an arrow-shaped bead, and a 6º on the wire.

2 On each end, string a rectangle bead, a 6º, an arrow, and a 6º. Repeat this pattern until the strand is within 3 in. (7.6cm) of the desired length.

3 **a** Determine the finished length of the beaded-link strand of your necklace. (This one is 31 in./79cm.) Subtract 2 in. (5cm) from that measurement, and cut that many 5-in. (13cm) pieces of beading wire. (This necklace uses 29 pieces.) To make a beaded link, string a crimp bead and 25 6ºs on one wire.

b Go through the crimp bead. On each side of the crimp bead, go through one or more 6ºs. Tighten the wires and crimp the crimp bead (see Basics, p. 12). Trim the excess wire.

BLACK
by popular

by **Jane Konkel**

demand

4 On another piece of beading wire, string a crimp bead and 25 6°s. Pass one end through the first beaded link. Repeat step 3b. Continue connecting links until the strand is within 6 in. of the desired length.

5 Cut a 10-in. (25cm) piece of beading wire. String a crimp bead and 25 6°s. Make a link, leaving a 5-in. wire tail on one end. Repeat on the other end.

6 Determine the finished length of the long strand of your necklace. (The long strand on this necklace is 39 in./ 1m.) Add 6 in. (15cm) and cut a piece of beading wire to that length. Center a 6°, a rectangle, and a 6° on the wire.

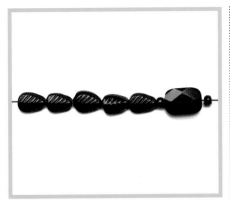

7 On each end, string five leaf-shaped beads, a 6º, a rectangle, and a 6º. Repeat this pattern until the strand is within 3 in. of the desired length.

1 earrings • String a 6º seed bead, a leaf-shaped bead, and a 6º on an eye pin. Make a plain loop (Basics) above the top bead, perpendicular to the bottom loop.

2 String a rectangle bead on an eye pin. Make a plain loop above the bead.

8 On the end of each strand, string approximately 1 in. (2.5cm) of 6ºs. String a crimp bead, a 6º, and the respective loop of half of the clasp. Go back through the last beads strung and tighten the wires. Check the fit, and add or remove beads from each end if necessary. Crimp the crimp beads, and trim the excess wire.

3 Open a loop on the rectangle unit and attach the leaf unit. Close the loop.

4 Open the loop on an earring wire and attach the dangle. Close the loop. Make a second earring to match the first. ❖

EDITOR'S TIPS
• For quick beaded links, line up separate rows of 25 seed beads in the channels of a bead-design board. Pick up beads with the tip of your beading wire, rather than stringing one bead at a time.
• For a different pattern, alternate the number of seed beads in each link. This will vary the size of your links.

Supply List

necklace
• **2** 16-in. (41cm) strands 10 x 14mm onyx rectangles (Rings & Things, 800-366-2156, rings-things.com)
• **2** 16-in. (41cm) strands 8 x 11mm black leaf-shaped beads (Rings & Things)
• **16–20** 9 x 18mm black arrow-shaped beads (Rings & Things)
• **50g** 6º black seed beads
• black flexible beading wire, .018 or .019
• **37 or more** gunmetal crimp beads
• three-strand clasp
• chainnose or crimping pliers
• diagonal wire cutters

earrings
• **2** 10 x 14mm onyx rectangles (Rings & Things)
• **2** 8 x 11mm black leaf-shaped beads (Rings & Things)
• **4** 6º black seed beads
• **4** 1½-in. (3.8cm) gunmetal eye pins
• pair of gunmetal earring wires (Rings & Things)
• chainnose pliers
• roundnose pliers
• diagonal wire cutters

Coral

Create a necklace and bracelet using clever substitutes for coral

The matte finish of coral highlighted with glossy crystals is a stunning combination. If you're opposed to using coral in your jewelry designs, red poppy jasper or sodalite are environmentally friendly substitutes. Sodalite's blue luster can easily be altered to mimic blue coral's denim shade. To achieve this faux finish, simply immerse sodalite beads in tarnish remover for about two minutes, air dry, then string these look-alikes with a clear conscience.

with a conscience

by Nancy Kugel

1 necklace • Determine the finished length of your necklace. (Both of these are 18 in./46cm.) Add 6 in. (15cm) and cut a piece of beading wire to that length. String a crimp bead, a bicone, and half of the clasp. Go back through the beads just strung and tighten the wire. Crimp the crimp bead (see Basics, p. 12).

2 String: bicone, round, bicone, pearl, bicone, round, bicone, cube. (Cover the wire's tail with the first few beads.) Repeat this pattern until the necklace is within 1 in. (2.5cm) of the desired length. End with a bicone.

3 String a crimp bead, a bicone, and the remaining half of the clasp. Go back through the last three beads strung and tighten the wire. Check the fit, and add or remove beads if necessary. Crimp the crimp bead, and trim the excess wire.

The designer offers kits for this project. See p. 255 for contact information.

1 bracelet • Determine the finished length of your bracelet. Add 5 in. (13cm) and cut a piece of beading wire to that length. String a crimp bead, a bicone, and half of the clasp. Go back through the beads just strung and tighten the wire. Crimp the crimp bead.

2 Follow steps 2 and 3 of the necklace, substituting rondelles for round beads and 6mm bicones for cubes, if desired. ✤

SupplyList

both projects
- flexible beading wire, .014 or .015
- chainnose or crimping pliers
- diagonal wire cutters
- Empire's Instant Tarnish Remover or Connoisseur's Silver Jewelry Cleaner (optional)

necklace
- 16-in. (41cm) strand 9mm coral, sodalite, or red jasper; rounds or rondelles
- **9–11** 6mm pearls
- **9–11** 4–6mm faceted crystal cubes
- **42–50** 4mm bicone crystals
- 2 crimp beads
- toggle clasp

bracelet
- **7–11** 9mm coral, sodalite, or red jasper; rounds or rondelles
- **3–5** 6mm pearls
- **3–5** 4–6mm faceted cube or bicone crystals
- **16–24** 4mm bicone crystals
- 2 crimp beads
- toggle clasp

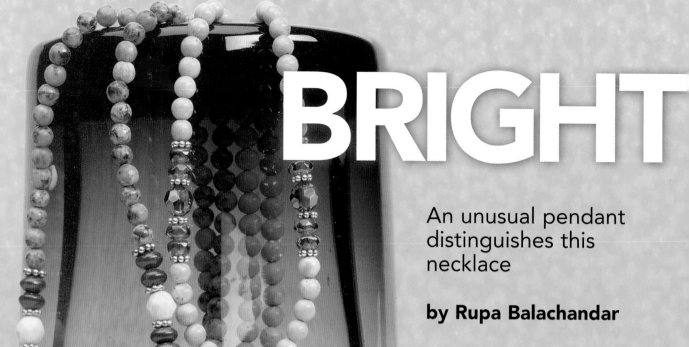

BRIGHT

An unusual pendant distinguishes this necklace

by Rupa Balachandar

Vivid blues and greens take flight in this bold feather necklace. Strung with turquoise, cobalt, brown, and lime green beads, it's the perfect accessory for your proud, brilliant self. If you're not one to strut, try a less-ostentatious version with a pheasant feather.

as a feather

1 Trim the feather to the desired shape and size, leaving ¼ in. (6.4mm) at the end of the quill. With the tip of your chainnose pliers, fold the quill's end. If the quill fits snugly in the crimp end, trim it to ⅛ in. (3mm) and do not fold it.

2 Insert the folded quill into a crimp end so the crimp end's loop is perpendicular to the feather. With chainnose pliers, flatten the middle section (crimp portion) of the crimp end (see Basics, p. 12).

3 Determine the finished length of your necklace. (Both of these are 16 in./ 41cm.) Add 6 in. (15cm) and cut a piece of beading wire to that length. Center the feather on the wire. String two spacers on each side.

4 On each end, string: six 4mm rounds, spacer, two rondelles, spacer, 6mm round, spacer, two rondelles, spacer.

SupplyList

- peacock feather (available at craft stores)
- 16-in. (41cm) strand 4mm round beads
- **2** 6mm faceted round beads
- **8** 5mm rondelles
- **2** 4mm bicone crystals
- **14** 4mm flat spacers
- flexible beading wire, .014 or .015
- crimp end with loop, with inner diameter to accommodate the feather's quill
- **2** crimp beads
- toggle clasp
- chainnose pliers
- diagonal wire cutters
- crimping pliers (optional)

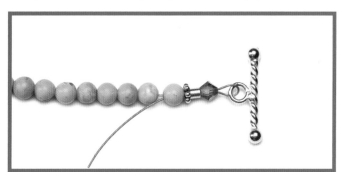

5 On each end, string 4mm rounds until the strand is within 1 in. (2.5cm) of the desired length.

On each end, string a spacer, a crimp bead, a bicone crystal, and half of the clasp. Go back through the last four beads and tighten the wires. Check the fit, and add or remove beads from each end if necessary. Crimp the crimp beads and trim the excess wire. ❖

Keeping tradition *alive*

Stamped and
seamed bench
beads shine in this
necklace and
earrings set

by Cathy Jakicic

The Thunderbird Supply Company is located on the Navajo reservation in Gallup, New Mexico. About 70 percent of its 80 employees are Native Americans. In fact, Thunderbird's production shop is staffed entirely by Native Americans, six of whom make stamped bench beads and seamed bench beads as well as many of the American Indian jewelry findings they sell. While Native American silversmithing and beading are fading arts, crafting jewelry is a multimillion-dollar industry that supports hundreds of families in the Gallup area.

1 **seam-bead necklace •** Determine the finished length of your necklace. (This one is 22 in./56cm.) Add 6 in. (15cm) and cut a piece of beading wire to that length. Using the four largest rondelles, center: rondelle, four seam beads, rondelle, blossom, rondelle, four seam beads, rondelle.

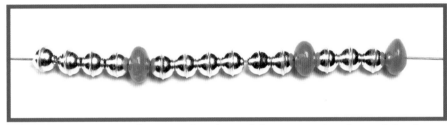

2 On each end, string: four seam beads, rondelle, six seam beads, rondelle, three seam beads, rondelle.

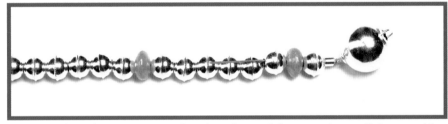

3 On each end, string six seam beads and a rondelle, repeating until the strand is within 1 in. (2.5cm) of the desired length.

On one end, string a seam bead, a crimp bead, and half of the clasp. Go back through the beads just strung and tighten the wire. Repeat on the other end. Check the fit, and add or remove beads from each end if necessary. Crimp the crimp beads (see Basics, p. 12), and trim the excess wire.

Supply List

seam-bead necklace
- 7mm sterling silver blossom (Thunderbird Supply Co., thunderbirdsupply.com)
- **90–100** 6mm sterling silver seam beads (Thunderbird Supply)
- **20** 4–10mm gemstone rondelles
- flexible beading wire, .014 or .015
- **2** crimp beads
- clasp
- chainnose or crimping pliers
- diagonal wire cutters

stamped-bead necklace
- **16** 6mm sterling silver stamped seam beads (Thunderbird Supply)
- 16-in. (41cm) strand 4–10mm gemstone rondelles
- flexible beading wire, .014 or .015
- **2** crimp beads
- sterling silver star button clasp (Thunderbird Supply)
- chainnose or crimping pliers
- diagonal wire cutters

earrings
- **4** 6mm sterling silver seam beads
- **20** 4–6mm gemstone rondelles
- **4** 1½-in. (3.8cm) head pins
- pair of earring wires
- chainnose pliers
- roundnose pliers
- diagonal wire cutters

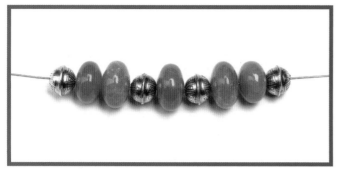

1 **stamped-bead necklace** • Determine the finished length of your necklace. (This one is 21 in./53cm.) Add 6 in. and cut a piece of beading wire to that length. Using the five largest rondelles, center: stamped bead, two rondelles, stamped bead, rondelle, stamped bead, two rondelles, stamped bead.

2 On each end, string four rondelles and a stamped bead. Repeat three times.
  On each end, string rondelles until the strand is within 1 in. of the desired length.

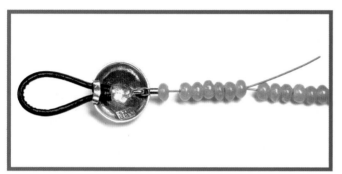

3 On one end, string a crimp bead and the loop end of the button clasp. Go back through the last few beads strung and tighten the wire.

4 Repeat on the other end with the remaining half of the clasp. Check the fit, and add or remove beads from each end if necessary. Crimp the crimp beads (Basics) and trim the excess wire.

1 **earrings** • On a head pin, string a rondelle, a seam bead, a rondelle, and a seam bead. Make a wrapped loop (Basics) above the top bead. On a second head pin, string eight rondelles. Make a wrapped loop above the top bead.

2 Open the loop of an earring wire and attach both dangles. Close the loop. Make a second earring to match the first. ❖

EDITOR'S TIPS
• See the editor's tip on p. 174 about working with graduated gemstone strands.
• Stamped seam beads can be substituted in the earring design.

Huetopia

Pale colors cluster in bubbly earrings • by Naomi Fujimoto

Enjoy a seaside palette with these trouble-free earrings. Combine a smattering of rondelles with mismatched larger rounds for a pleasing asymmetry. The quiet hues will provide a pretty and understated accent to your wardrobe.

EDITOR'S TIP
Prefer smaller earrings? String just five bead units on each 2½-in. (6.4cm) head pin.

1 To make a bead unit: String a rondelle on a 1-in. (2.5cm) head pin. Make a plain loop (see Basics, p. 12) above the bead. Make a total of nine bead units.

2 On a 2½-in. (6.4cm) head pin, string a round crystal, nine bead units, and a rondelle. Make a wrapped loop (Basics) above the bead.

3 Open the loop of an earring wire and attach the dangle. Close the loop. Make a second earring. Use a complementary crystal color if desired. ✤

SupplyList

- **2** 12mm round faceted glass or gemstones
- **20** 3–4mm faceted glass rondelles
- **18** 1-in. (2.5cm) 22-gauge head pins
- **2** 2½-in. (6.4cm) 22-gauge head pins
- pair of earring wires
- chainnose pliers
- roundnose pliers
- diagonal wire cutters

Showcase gorgeous green beads
in a classic three-strand necklace

Green

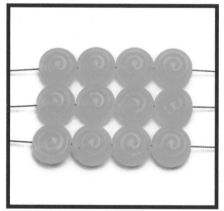

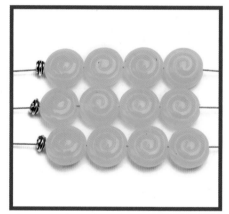

1 **a** Determine the finished length of your necklace. (The shortest strand of this necklace is 14 in./36cm.) Add 6 in. (15cm) and cut a piece of beading wire to that length. Cut two more pieces, each 2 in. (5cm) longer than the previous piece.

b Center four round beads on each wire.

2 On each end, string a 5mm spacer and four round beads. Repeat this pattern until the strand is within 1 in. (2.5cm) of the desired length.

3 On each end, string a 4mm spacer, a crimp bead, a spacer, and the respective loop of half of the clasp. Go back through the beads just strung and tighten the wires. Check the fit, and add or remove beads if necessary. Crimp the crimp beads (see Basics, p. 12) and trim the excess wire. ❖

EDITOR'S TIP
If your wardrobe does not scream for green, try a different bead color. Look for beads that are similar in size and shape to M&M candies.

Supply List

- **3–4** 16-in. (41cm) strands 12–14mm flat round beads
- **18–24** 5mm spacers
- **12** 4mm spacers
- flexible beading wire, .014 or .015
- **6** crimp beads
- three-strand clasp with chain extender
- chainnose or crimping pliers
- diagonal wire cutters

piece

by Diana Grossman

Who says it's not easy being green?
Get back to nature by stringing
multiple strands of verdant beads
in this collar-style necklace. For
added variety, sprinkle with gold or
silver spacers. Your necklace will
provide a fresh splash of green as
well as a touch of elegance
to your wardrobe.

Weighing
IN

Offset gemstone
rondelles with
tiny crystals for a
necklace of substance

by Naomi Fujimoto

Tip the scales in your favor with a nicely balanced necklace of pink opal rondelles. Tiny crystals in shades of pink, peach, and khaki enhance the variegated gemstones. You don't need to string the crystals in any particular order; simply alternate the rondelles with miniature punches of color. A jewel-encrusted clasp adds a harmonious finish.

SupplyList

- 16-in. (41cm) strand 6 x 9mm faceted pink opal rondelles (Art Gems, artgemsinc.com)
- **50–60** 3mm bicone crystals
- flexible beading wire, .014 or .015
- **2** crimp beads
- toggle clasp (clasp with crystals available from Eclectica, 262-641-0910)
- chainnose or crimping pliers
- diagonal wire cutters

1 Determine the finished length of your necklace. (This one is 16 in./41cm.) Add 6 in. (15cm) and cut a piece of beading wire to that length. Organize your crystals by color.

2 Select a rondelle for the center of the necklace and two crystals that highlight the colors in the rondelle. String one crystal, the rondelle, and the other crystal on the wire. Center the beads.

EDITOR'S TIP
Before stringing, remove all the pink opal rondelles from the strand. String the deepest-colored opals at the center of the necklace.

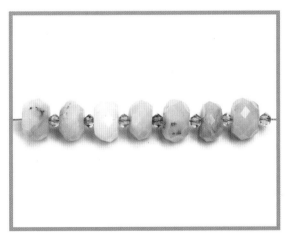

3 String a rondelle and a crystal on each end, repeating until the necklace is within 1 in. (2.5cm) of the desired length. End with a crystal.

4 On each end, string a crimp bead, a crystal, and half of the clasp. Go back through the last three beads strung and tighten the wire. Check the fit, and add or remove beads from each end if necessary. Crimp the crimp beads (see Basics, p. 12), and trim the excess wire. ✤

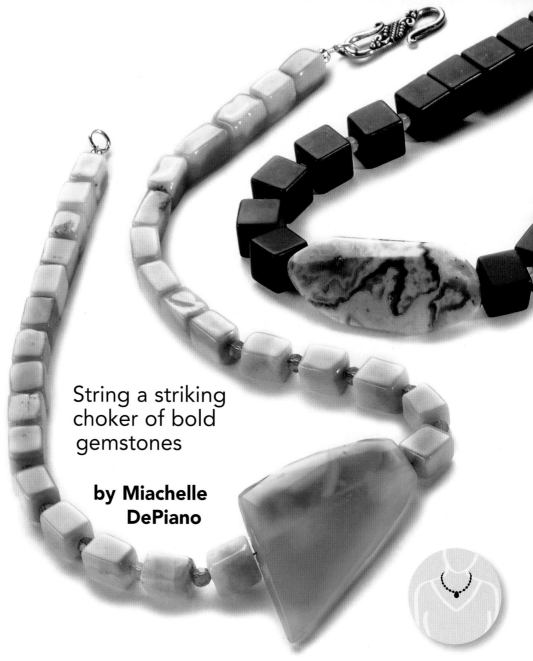

Playing all the angles

String a striking choker of bold gemstones

by Miachelle DePiano

Create drama with a simple stringing project by combining elements that, because of their color or shape – or both – spark interesting visual tension. In this piece, an irregularly shaped nugget surrounded by the right angles of square or rectangular beads is an unexpected and dynamic combination.

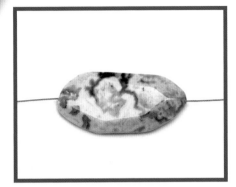

1 necklace • Determine the finished length of your necklace. (These are 17 in./43cm.) Add 6 in. (15cm) and cut a piece of beading wire to that length. Center the nugget on the wire.

2 On each end, string a square or rectangular bead and a crystal. Repeat the pattern four more times.

On each end, string square or rectangular beads until the necklace is within 2 in. (5cm) of the desired length.

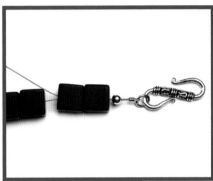

3 On each end, string a spacer, a crimp bead, and a jump ring. Go back through the last beads strung and tighten the wire. Check the fit, and add or remove an equal number of beads from each end if necessary. Crimp the crimp beads (see Basics, p. 12) and trim the excess wire. Attach the clasp to one of the jump rings.

SUPPLY NOTE
Some S-hook clasps come with a soldered jump ring already attached. In that case, you only need an S-hook clasp with one soldered jump ring.

earrings • On a head pin, string a square or rectangular bead and a crystal. Make a wrapped loop above the crystal (Basics). Open the loop on an earring wire and attach the dangle. Close the loop. Make a second earring to match the first. ❖

SupplyList

necklace
- 40–50mm nugget, irregularly shaped
- **28–34** 10mm square or rectangular beads
- **10** 4mm round crystals
- **2** round spacers
- flexible beading wire, .014 or .015
- **2** crimp beads
- S-hook clasp with **2** soldered jump rings
- chainnose pliers
- roundnose pliers
- crimping pliers (optional)
- diagonal wire cutters

earrings
- **2** 10mm square or rectangular beads
- **2** 4mm round crystals
- **2** 2-in. (5cm) head pins
- pair of earring wires
- chainnose pliers
- roundnose pliers
- diagonal wire cutters

by Rupa Balachandar

A strand of graduated rondelles creates a wave of color

A richly colored strand of gemstones needs little embellishment. Keep it simple with just a few metallic accents in the front, and let the subtle flow of graduated stones move all eyes to where they belong – on you. A pair of equally subtle earrings uses the interplay between the gemstones and the accents to complete the look.

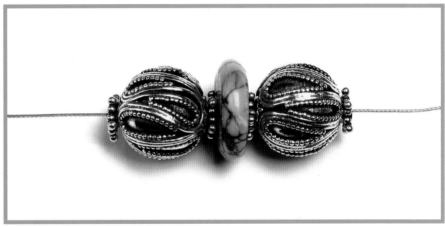

1 **necklace** • Determine the finished length of your necklace. (These are 19 in./ 48cm.) Add 6 in. (15cm) and cut a piece of beading wire to that length. String: 8mm spacer, 18mm metal bead, 8mm spacer, largest rondelle, 8mm spacer, 18mm, 8mm spacer. Center the beads on the wire.

2 On each end, string the next-largest rondelle, two 8mm spacers, the next-largest rondelle, and two 8mm spacers.

3 On each end, string rondelles in descending size until the necklace is within 1 in. (2.5cm) of the desired length. (Set aside two of the smallest rondelles if you're planning to make matching earrings.) On each end, string: 4mm spacer, 3mm spacer, crimp bead, 3mm spacer, half of the clasp. Go back through the beads just strung, and tighten the wire. Check the fit, and add or remove beads from each end if necessary. Crimp the crimp beads (see Basics, p. 12), and trim the excess wire.

1 **earrings** • String a rondelle and an 18mm metal bead on a head pin. Make the first half of a wrapped loop (Basics) above the bead.

2 Attach the dangle to the loop of an earring thread. Complete the wraps. Make a second earring to match the first. ❖

Supply List

necklace
- 16-in. (41cm) strand graduated gemstone rondelles, 6–18mm (Fire Mountain Gems, 800-355-2137, firemountaingems.com)
- **2** 18mm round metal beads
- **12** 8mm flat spacers
- **2** 4mm flat spacers
- **4** 3mm spacers
- flexible beading wire, .014 or .015
- **2** crimp beads
- toggle clasp
- chainnose or crimping pliers
- diagonal wire cutters

earrings
- **2** 6mm rondelles, left over from necklace
- **2** 18mm round metal beads
- **2** 2-in. (5cm) head pins
- pair of earring threads
- chainnose pliers
- roundnose pliers
- diagonal wire cutters

Shortcuts

Readers' tips to make your beading life easier

1 smooth finish
When finishing a strung necklace or bracelet, dab the end of the flexible beading wire with hand lotion. The wire will go back through the beads more easily.
– *Laura Bub,*
East Granby, Conn.

2 pitcher perfect
For a pretty and functional jewelry display, hang earrings on the rim of a pitcher, mug, bowl, or vase. (The wider the rim, the more pairs you can hang.) The inside of the container can hold earrings that need repair or have lost their mates.
– *Amanda Bohm,*
Austin, Texas

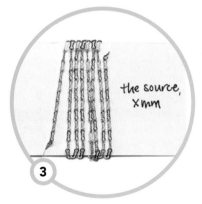

3 storing chain
To prevent fine chain from tangling, keep it on a business card. Cut two notches at opposite edges of the card, wrap the chain around, and secure the ends in the notches. Label the card with the vendor's name, the size of the chain, and the item number.
– *D. Harris, via e-mail*

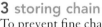

the source, Xmm

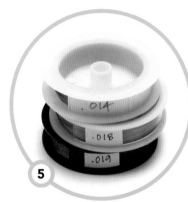

4 box of chocolates
After you finish that Valentine's Day box of chocolates, clean the plastic tray and use it to sort beads. The tray holds small quantities of many kinds of beads and findings, which is helpful when stringing a complicated piece.
– *Samantha Bond,*
via e-mail

5 wire at a glance
I like to organize spools of flexible beading wire in stacks but want to know their sizes without removing each spool. The solution: Label each spool's plastic cuff with the wire's diameter. Use a permanent marker, and a small white sticker for black or clear plastic. You'll see each wire's thickness at a glance.
– *R. Podell, Milwaukee, Wis.*

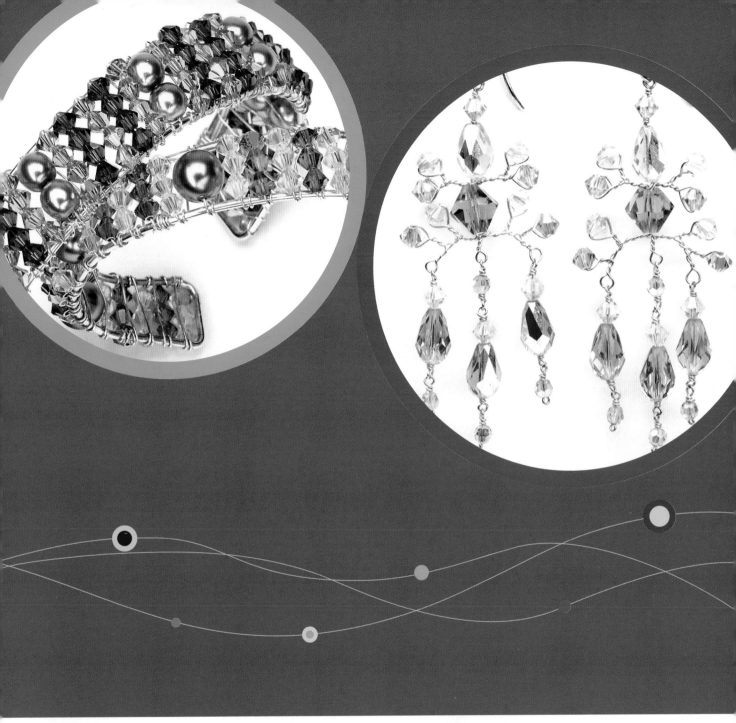

Crystals

Arrange a
bouquet
centerpiece
for a crystal
necklace

Petal pusher

by Eva Kapitany

At the heart of this vibrant crystal strand is a lovely spray of lush flower beads. Bring in spring by first selecting glass blossoms. Then, add jeweled head pins for extra sparkle. Finally, choose crystals in a monochromatic color scheme or in the two colors most prevalent in the flowers.

1 String a 6mm bicone crystal and a flower-shaped bead on a crystal head pin. Make a wrapped loop (see Basics, p. 12) above the top bead. Make a total of six flower-bead units.

2 On a head pin, string an 8mm cube crystal and each flower-bead unit. Make a wrapped loop above the top bead unit. Continue wrapping the wire over and around the loops of the attached bead units.

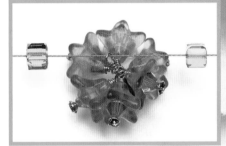

3 Determine the finished length of your necklace. (These are 17 in./ 43cm.) Add 6 in. (15cm), and cut a piece of beading wire to that length. String a 6mm cube crystal, the bouquet pendant, and a 6mm cube. Center the beads on the wire.

SupplyList

- **6** 9 x 14mm flower-shaped beads
- **9–13** 8mm cube crystals
- **2** 6mm cube crystals
- **30–42** 6mm round crystals
- **6** 6mm bicone crystals
- **40–56** 4mm bicone crystals
- flexible beading wire, .014 or .015
- **7** crystal head pins (jewelrysupply.com)
- **2** crimp beads
- toggle clasp
- chainnose pliers
- roundnose pliers
- diagonal wire cutters
- crimping pliers (optional)

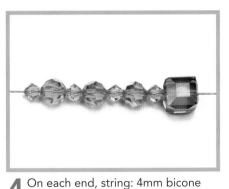

4 On each end, string: 4mm bicone crystal, round crystal, 4mm bicone, round, 4mm bicone, round, 4mm bicone, 8mm cube. Repeat until the strand is within 1 in. (2.5cm) of the desired length.

5 On each end, string a crimp bead, a 4mm bicone, and half of the clasp. Go back through the last three beads strung and tighten the wire. Check the fit, and add or remove beads from each end if necessary. Crimp the crimp beads (Basics) and trim the excess wire. ❖

Crystal cascade

by Irina Miech

A circular etched pendant punctuates falling crystal clusters on this necklace. Ear threads overflow with matching sparklers to complete a dainty duo. These crystals, attached to chain with wrapped loops, give a glimmer of shimmer to ease you gracefully through your next special occasion.

Link crystals to a chain and ear threads for a feminine necklace and earrings

1 necklace • Cut a 4-in. (10cm) piece of wire. Make the first half of a wrapped loop (see Basics, p. 12) 1½ in. (3.8cm) from one end of the wire. Make the loop large enough to accommodate the pendant. Attach the pendant and complete the wraps.

EDITOR'S TIP

When attaching beads or crystals to chain links, temporarily string a head pin through the chain's top link. Lift the chain off your work surface and hold it up by the head pin to check that the beads hang evenly.

2 String a bicone crystal on a head pin. Make the first half of a wrapped loop (Basics) above the crystal. Make a total of 12–14 bicone units.

3 Cut a 1-in. (2.5cm) piece of chain. Attach a bicone unit to the chain's bottom link and complete the wraps. Attach each remaining bicone unit to a link, spacing them evenly along the chain.

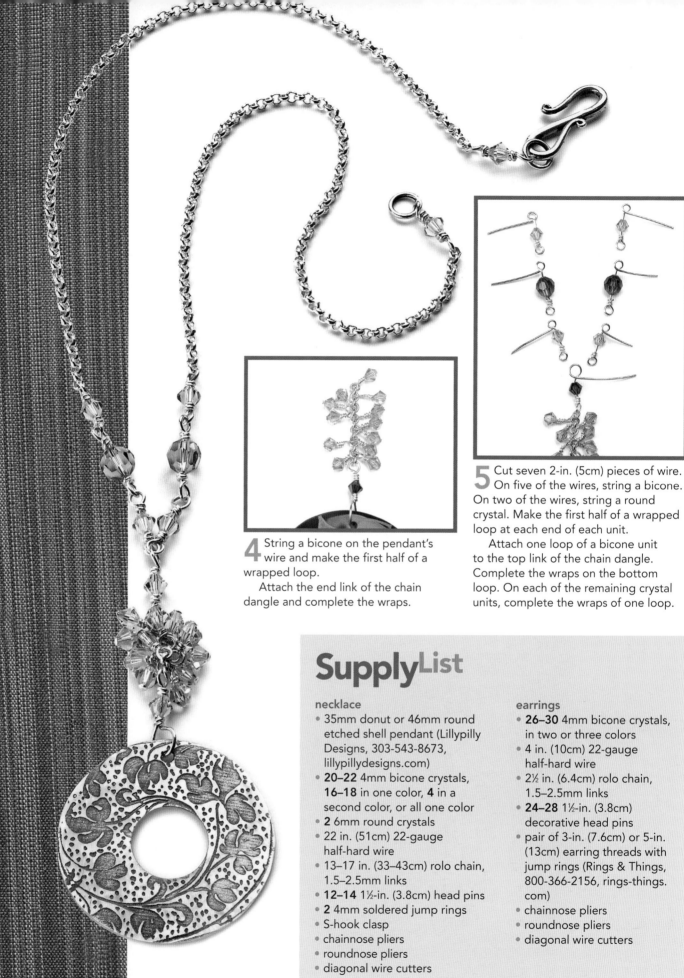

4 String a bicone on the pendant's wire and make the first half of a wrapped loop.

Attach the end link of the chain dangle and complete the wraps.

5 Cut seven 2-in. (5cm) pieces of wire. On five of the wires, string a bicone. On two of the wires, string a round crystal. Make the first half of a wrapped loop at each end of each unit.

Attach one loop of a bicone unit to the top link of the chain dangle. Complete the wraps on the bottom loop. On each of the remaining crystal units, complete the wraps of one loop.

Supply List

necklace
- 35mm donut or 46mm round etched shell pendant (Lillypilly Designs, 303-543-8673, lillypillydesigns.com)
- **20–22** 4mm bicone crystals, **16–18** in one color, **4** in a second color, or all one color
- 2 6mm round crystals
- 22 in. (51cm) 22-gauge half-hard wire
- 13–17 in. (33–43cm) rolo chain, 1.5–2.5mm links
- **12–14** 1½-in. (3.8cm) head pins
- 2 4mm soldered jump rings
- S-hook clasp
- chainnose pliers
- roundnose pliers
- diagonal wire cutters

earrings
- **26–30** 4mm bicone crystals, in two or three colors
- 4 in. (10cm) 22-gauge half-hard wire
- 2½ in. (6.4cm) rolo chain, 1.5–2.5mm links
- **24–28** 1½-in. (3.8cm) decorative head pins
- pair of 3-in. (7.6cm) or 5-in. (13cm) earring threads with jump rings (Rings & Things, 800-366-2156, rings-things.com)
- chainnose pliers
- roundnose pliers
- diagonal wire cutters

7 Cut two 2-in. pieces of wire. On each wire, string a bicone crystal and make the first half of a wrapped loop at each end.

8 Attach one loop of each bicone unit to each remaining end link of chain.
Attach each remaining loop to a jump ring. Complete the wraps. Attach each jump ring to one end of the S-hook clasp.

6 Attach the top loop of the pendant unit to the wrapped loops of two bicone units. Complete the wraps. Attach each remaining unit's loop to the wrapped loop of the crystal unit above it as shown, and complete the wraps.

Cut two 6-in. (15cm) or longer pieces of chain. On the end link of each, attach the loop of a bicone unit and complete the wraps.

Check the fit, allowing 1½ in. for finishing. Trim an equal number of chain links from each end, if necessary.

1 earrings • String a bicone on a decorative head pin. Make the first half of a wrapped loop above the crystal. Make a total of 12–14 bicone units in two or three colors.

2 Cut a 1-in. piece of chain. Attach a bicone unit to the chain's end link and complete the wraps. Attach each remaining unit to each link, alternating colors.

3 Cut a 2-in. piece of wire. String a bicone and make the first half of a wrapped loop at each end.

Attach one loop to the end link of the chain dangle and the other loop to an ear thread's jump ring. Complete the wraps. Make a second earring to match the first. ❖

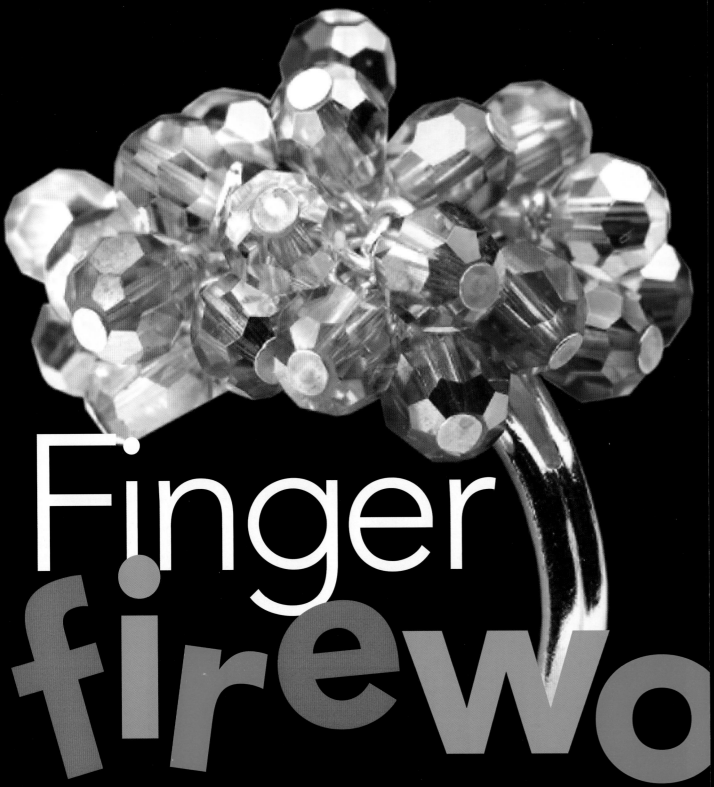

Finger firewo

Create some excitement with this kinetic sparkler

Who says attaining goals has to be drudgery? Resolve to use up your leftover crystals, practice your wrapped loops, and just get more movement into your day. Making this quick and easy ring lets you check all three off your list. Your reward for this industriousness? A ring that captures the light – as well as the oohs and ahhs – when the crystals sway with every movement of your hand.

1 String each crystal on a head pin. Make the first half of a wrapped loop above each crystal (see Basics, p. 12).

2 Attach a crystal unit to one of the outer loops on the ring form. Complete the wraps.

3 Attach a crystal unit to each of the remaining loops on one row of the ring form. Attach a second crystal unit to each loop in that row. Attach a third crystal unit, then a fourth, to each loop. Complete the wraps.

4 Repeat steps 2 and 3 on the second row of the ring form. If using multiple crystal colors, alternate the order in which you attach them to each loop. ❖

by Sue Godfrey and Gail Wing

EDITOR'S TIP
Try this design with tiny pearls for a soft, elegant glow. Or substitute several 3mm beads for added interest.

Supply List

- **32** 4mm crystals
- eight-loop ring form (Midwest Beads, 262-781-7670, beaderschoice.com)
- **32** 1½-in. (3.8cm) head pins
- chainnose pliers
- roundnose pliers
- diagonal wire cutters

Sweeping statement

by Todd Canyon Sinclair

Assorted beads combine with metal rings in long, lanky earrings

Don a pair of these long, 3½-inch earrings to get everybody talking. More than just an outfit's sidekick, mismatched dangles express your free spirit. They're heavy on style but light on your lobes. So make a bold statement and relish the comments!

SupplyList

- **4** oval beads, approximately 7 x 9mm
- **4–10** 6mm bicone crystals
- **7–15** 4mm bicone crystals, in two colors
- **10–15** 4mm round Czech fire-polished beads
- 1g 11º seed beads
- **4** 9mm metal rings
- 8 in. (20cm) half-hard 24-gauge wire
- **6** 1½-in. (3.8cm) head pins
- pair of earring wires
- chainnose pliers
- roundnose pliers
- diagonal wire cutters

1 Cut two 2-in. (5cm) pieces of 24-gauge wire. On the end of one wire, make a plain loop (see Basics, p. 12). String: oval bead, 11º seed bead, round crystal, 11º, 4mm bicone, 11º. Make a plain loop perpendicular to the first loop. On the other wire, make a plain loop at one end. String: 6mm bicone, 11º, oval bead, 11º, 6mm bicone. Make a plain loop above the crystal, parallel to the first loop.

2 To make a dangle, string a pattern of three crystals and 11ºs on a 1½-in. (3.8cm) head pin. Make a plain loop above the top bead. Make two more dangles, stringing an alternating pattern of three crystals and 11ºs. If desired, string different patterns for each dangle. Make a total of three crystal dangles.

3 Open the loop on a dangle and attach it to a metal ring. Close the loop. Attach the remaining crystal dangles to the ring.

4 Open the bottom loop on the perpendicular-loop unit from step 1. Attach a metal ring and close the loop. Open a loop on the remaining bead unit from step 1 and attach it to the metal ring. Close the loop.

5 Attach the metal ring with three dangles to the bottom loop of the bead unit from step 4.

6 Open an earring wire. Attach the bead unit's remaining loop. Close the earring wire loop.

Make a second earring to match the first. ✤

EDITOR'S TIP
For extra security, make wrapped loops (instead of plain loops) to connect each bead unit and dangle: Use six 2½-in. (6.4cm) head pins and four 3-in. (7.6cm) pieces of 24-gauge wire for the bead units.

Celebrate sunny days with a fresh silver, briolette, and crystal necklace

Bright

Adorn yourself with a feminine, floral necklace. A bold silver flower commands attention, while briolettes splay in luscious petals around your neck. Like real flowers, this necklace's fresh colors will bring beauty and a joyful outlook no matter what the weather.

1 Determine the finished length of your necklace. (The yellow necklace is 15½ in./39.4cm; the aqua necklace, 16½ in./41.9cm.) Add 6 in. (15cm) and cut a piece of beading wire to that length. Center a 4–5mm round spacer, the pendant, and a spacer on the wire.

2 On each end, string a 4mm bicone crystal, a 6 or 8mm round crystal, a bicone, and two briolettes. Repeat, using 8mm round crystals, until the necklace is within 1 in. (2.5cm) of the desired length.

by Katee Lee Chimpouras

beauty

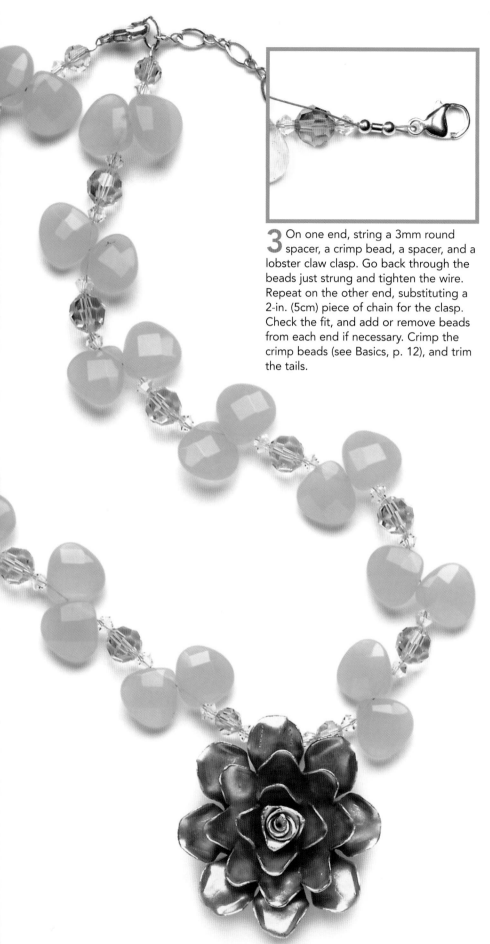

3 On one end, string a 3mm round spacer, a crimp bead, a spacer, and a lobster claw clasp. Go back through the beads just strung and tighten the wire. Repeat on the other end, substituting a 2-in. (5cm) piece of chain for the clasp. Check the fit, and add or remove beads from each end if necessary. Crimp the crimp beads (see Basics, p. 12), and trim the tails.

4 String an 8mm round crystal on a head pin and make the first half of a wrapped loop (Basics). Attach the loop to the chain and complete the wraps. ✤

EDITOR'S TIPS

• Briolettes are typically sold in 16-in. (41cm) or shorter strands, strung with plastic spacers between each bead. One 16-in. (41cm) strand has enough beads for a 17-in. (43cm) necklace. While a chain extender is usually optional, definitely include one if you want a longer necklace.
• For matching earrings, skip the briolettes and opt for simple silver and crystal drops.

Supply List

- pendant with loop on back, approximately 45mm
- 16-in. (41cm) strand 13mm briolettes
- **15–17** 8mm round crystals
- **2** 6mm round crystals (optional)
- **28–32** 4mm bicone crystals
- **2** 4–5mm round spacers
- **4** 3mm round spacers
- flexible beading wire, .014 or .015
- 1½-in. (3.8cm) head pin
- **2** crimp beads
- lobster claw clasp
- 2 in. (5cm) chain for extender, 5–6mm links
- chainnose pliers
- roundnose pliers
- diagonal wire cutters
- crimping pliers (optional)

Drops of light

Delicate briolette-teardrop earrings will make a splash

by Lea Rose Nowicki

Drops of light, like tears of joy, are an unexpected pleasure. These lovely earrings use minimal time and materials to maximum effect. In no time at all, you can make a flood of teardrops that are sure to bring joy.

SupplyList

- **2** 13mm German-crystal briolettes, top drilled (Midwest Beads, 262-781-7670, beaderschoice.com)
- **2** 6mm button crystals
- **2** 4mm bicone crystals
- 4 in. (10cm) 24-gauge half-hard wire
- 2½ in. (6.4cm) chain, 2–3mm links
- **2** 4mm jump rings
- pair of earring wires
- chainnose pliers
- roundnose pliers
- diagonal wire cutters

1 Cut two 1-in. (2.5cm) pieces of wire. On one wire, make a plain loop (see Basics, p. 12) at one end. String a button crystal and make a plain loop above the crystal. On the other wire, make a plain loop at one end. String a bicone crystal and make a plain loop above the crystal.

2 Open a jump ring (Basics). String a crystal briolette.

3 Cut two ½-in. (1.3cm) pieces of chain. Attach one piece to the briolette unit. Close the jump ring. Open a plain loop on the button unit and attach the other end of the chain. Close the loop. Open the other loop on the button unit and attach the second piece of chain. Close the loop. Attach the bicone unit to the chain. Open the loop on an earring wire. Attach the dangle and close the loop. Make a second earring to match the first. ❖

Flash flood

Crystals and liquid silver or gold make waves in a multistrand necklace

by Sue Godfrey

A current of liquid silver is a fluid base for a rainbow of crystals. Or, choose an alternate colorway that floats a monochromatic assortment on a wave of liquid gold.

Design Guidelines

• For the silver necklace, use assorted colors of 4mm bicone crystals. (Mixes are available from Knot Just Beads, 414-771-8360, orders@knotjustbeads.com.) You'll need 130–150 crystals.
• For the gold necklace, use 4mm Swarovski crystals in the following colors and quantities:

 45–50 padparadscha bicone crystals

 25–30 Indian-red round crystals

 20–25 light-Colorado-topaz AB round crystals

 15–20 Ceylon-topaz bicone crystals

 15–20 light-peach-satin bicone crystals

SupplyList

• **120–150** 4mm crystals (see Design Guidelines for suggestions)
• **10** 3mm bicone crystals (for silver rainbow necklace)
• 12g liquid-gold beads, (beadFX, beadfx.com) or 10g liquid-silver beads (Rio Grande, 800-545-6566)
• 5g 13º seed beads (for silver rainbow necklace)
• flexible beading wire, .014 or .015
• **10** crimp beads
• **2** 4mm soldered jump rings
• 4mm jump ring
• 4mm split ring
• lobster claw clasp
• chainnose pliers
• roundnose pliers
• diagonal wire cutters
• crimping pliers (optional)

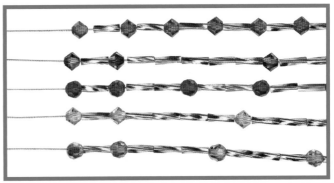

1a silver rainbow necklace • Determine the finished length of your necklace. (This one is 17½ in./44.5cm.) Add 6 in. (15cm) and cut five pieces of beading wire to that length. Tape one end of each wire. On one wire, string two liquid-silver beads, a 13º seed bead, a 4mm bicone crystal, and a 13º. Repeat until the strand is within 1 in. (2.5cm) of the desired length, ending with two liquid-silver beads. Tape the end.

b On the second wire, string three liquid-silver beads, a 13º, a 4mm bicone, and a 13º. Repeat until the strand is within 1 in. of the desired length, ending with three liquid-silver beads. Tape the end.

c On the third wire, string five liquid-silver beads, a 13º, a 4mm bicone, and a 13º. Repeat until the strand is within 1 in. of the desired length, ending with five liquid-silver beads. Tape the end.

d On the fourth wire, string seven liquid-silver beads, a 13º, a 4mm bicone, and a 13º. Repeat until the strand is within 1 in. of the desired length, ending with seven liquid-silver beads. Tape the end.

e On the fifth wire, string eight liquid-silver beads, a 13º, a 4mm bicone, and a 13º. Repeat until the strand is within 1 in. of the desired length, ending with eight liquid-silver beads. Tape the end.

1a gold necklace • Determine the finished length of your necklace. (This one is 17½ in./44.5cm.) Add 6 in. (15cm) and cut five pieces of beading wire to that length. On one wire, string a padparadscha crystal and a liquid-gold bead. Repeat until the strand is within 1 in. (2.5cm) of the desired length, ending with a crystal. Tape the ends.

b On the second wire, string a light-peach-satin crystal and five gold beads. Repeat until the strand is within 1½ in. (3.8cm) of the desired length, ending with a crystal. String a gold bead and a crystal on each end. Tape the ends.

c On the third wire, string an Indian-red crystal and two gold beads. Repeat until the strand is within 1½ in. of the desired length, ending with a crystal. String a gold bead and a crystal on each end. Tape the ends.

d On the fourth wire, string a Ceylon-topaz crystal and four gold beads. Repeat until the strand is within 1½ in. of the desired length, ending with a crystal. String a gold bead and a crystal on each end. Tape the ends.

e On the fifth wire, string a light-Colorado-topaz AB crystal and three gold beads. Repeat until the strand is within 1 in. of the desired length, ending with a crystal. String a gold bead and a crystal on each end. Tape the ends.

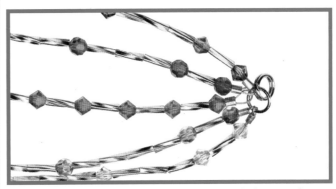

2a Arrange the strands as desired. Remove the tape from one end of a strand. String a 13º, a 3mm bicone, a crimp bead, a 13º, and a soldered jump ring. Go back through the last three beads and tighten the wire. Repeat with the remaining strands, attaching all the ends on each side to a single jump ring. Check the fit, and add or remove beads from each end if necessary. Crimp the crimp beads (see Basics, p. 12) and trim the excess wire.

b Attach a split ring to one of the soldered jump rings. Open a jump ring (Basics) and attach a clasp to the other soldered jump ring. Close the jump ring.

2a Arrange the strands as desired. Remove the tape from the end of one strand. String a crimp bead and a soldered jump ring. Go back through the last three beads and tighten the wire. Repeat on the other end. Repeat with the remaining strands, attaching all the ends on each side to a single jump ring. Check the fit, and add or remove beads from each end if necessary. Crimp the crimp beads and trim the excess wire.

b Attach a split ring to one of the soldered jump rings. Open a jump ring and attach a clasp to the other soldered jump ring. Close the jump ring. ❖

Double

This combination
of crystals and
curved tube
beads can be
worn as a
necklace or as
a bracelet

Wear your art on your sleeve – or around your neck. As a necklace, it's an elegant, single strand, but its impact multiplies when it's wound around your wrist. Simple earrings are a perfect match however you decide to wear your creation. But why choose? This versatile piece is so quick and easy to make, you'll want at least two.

play

by Amy DeLeo and Lindsay O. Vance

SupplyList

necklace/bracelet
- **38–49** 17.4 x 2.5mm curved tube beads (Rio Grande, 800-545-6566)
- **39–50** 4mm bicone crystals
- flexible beading wire, .014 or .015
- **2** crimp beads (Twisted Tornado crimp beads available at Via Murano, viamurano.com)
- lobster claw clasp and soldered jump ring
- chainnose pliers
- diagonal wire cutters

earrings
- **2** 17.4 x 2.5mm curved tube beads (Rio Grande)
- **4** 4mm bicone crystals
- **2** 2-in. (5cm) head pins
- pair of earring wires
- chainnose pliers
- roundnose pliers
- diagonal wire cutters

1 necklace/bracelet • Determine the finished length of your necklace/bracelet. It should loop around your wrist four times. (This one is 32 in./81cm.) Double that measurement (the curved beads will take up extra wire) and cut a piece of beading wire to that length. String an alternating pattern of bicone crystals and curved tube beads, beginning and ending with a crystal.

2 On one end, string a crimp bead and the clasp. Go back through the crimp bead and the crystal, and tighten the wire. Repeat on the other end, substituting a jump ring for the clasp. Check the fit, and add or remove beads if necessary. Making sure the wires are side by side, flatten the crimp bead (see Basics, p. 12). Turn the crimp bead over and flatten it again. Repeat on the other end.

> **EDITOR'S TIP**
> Twisted Tornado crimp beads create a secure hold because their texture grips the beading wire. Crimping pliers are not necessary.

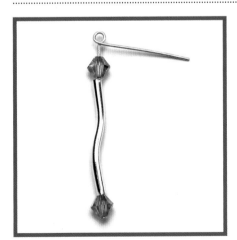

1 earrings • On a 2-in. (5cm) head pin, string a bicone crystal, a curved tube bead, and a crystal. Make the first half of a wrapped loop above the crystal (Basics).

2 Attach the dangle to the loop on an earring wire. Complete the wraps. Make a second earring to match the first. ❖

Loops & ladders

Play with shapes
and colors to create
a stylish choker

by Catherine Hodge

This ladder pendant is a
cinch to make, and you'll
love its easy sparkle and
sophistication. The neck
wire and clasp are handmade,
but don't fret – the personal
touches won't slow your
stylish climb a bit.

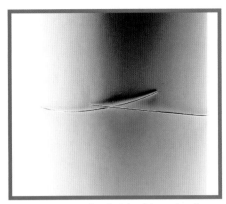

1 Determine the finished length of your necklace. (These are 16 in./41cm.) Add 3 in. (7.6cm) and cut a piece of 18-gauge wire to that length.
Wrap the wire around a round object, such as an oatmeal container.

2 On a head pin, string: color A bicone crystal, outer hole of a spacer bar, color B bicone, color C cube crystal, outer hole of a spacer bar, color A bicone, color A cube, outer hole of a spacer bar, color B bicone, color C cube. Make a wrapped loop (see Basics, p. 12) above the top crystal.

3 On a head pin, string: color B bicone, color C cube, middle hole of a spacer bar, color A bicone, color A cube, middle hole of a spacer bar, color B bicone, color C cube, middle hole of a spacer bar, color A bicone, color A cube. Make a wrapped loop above the top crystal.

4 Repeat step 2, stringing the remaining holes of the spacer bars. Center the pendant on the neck wire.

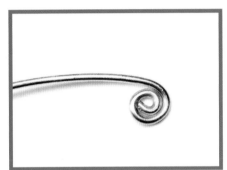

5 Grasp one end of the wire with the tip of your roundnose pliers, and form a small loop that curls toward the inside of the neck wire. Continue to make coils with your fingers, holding the wire with chainnose pliers, until you have formed a spiral.

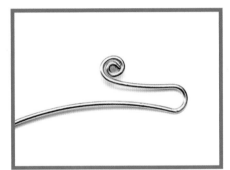

6 About ¾ in. (1.9cm) from the spiral, grip the wire with the widest part of your roundnose pliers. Bring the wire around the top jaw of the pliers to make a hook.

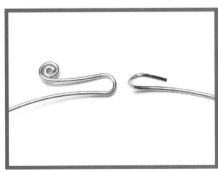

7 About ¼ in. (6mm) from the other end of the wire, grip the wire with the widest part of your roundnose pliers. Roll the wire to form an open loop perpendicular to the hook. File the end if necessary. ❖

Supply List

- **12** 4mm bicone crystals, **6** color A, **6** color B
- **10** 4mm cube crystals, **4** color A, **6** color C
- **3** 11–13mm three-hole spacer bars
- 18–22 in. (46–56cm) 18-gauge half-hard wire
- **3** 2½-in. (6.4cm) head pins
- chainnose pliers
- roundnose pliers
- diagonal wire cutters
- metal file (optional)

What's an alternative and ingenious technique that allows you to make hoop earrings without standard hoop findings? Use beading wire. The flexibility gives you the option to make not only a double hoop design, but earrings in virtually any size. String a combination of crystals, spacers, and seed beads, or experiment with a bead mix of your own.

Full circle

String crystal hoop earrings with ease

by Shruti Gautam Dev

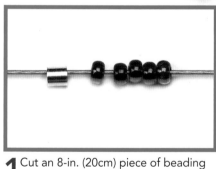

1 Cut an 8-in. (20cm) piece of beading wire. Tape one end of the wire, leaving a 1½-in. (3.8cm) tail. String a crimp bead and five 11º seed beads.

2 String a flat spacer, a crystal, a spacer, and an 11º. Repeat this pattern six more times.

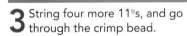

3 String four more 11ºs, and go through the crimp bead.

4 String five 11ºs, and repeat the pattern in step 2 three times.

5 String four more 11ºs. Go through the crimp bead and the adjacent 11º. Remove the tape from the wire's end and go through the bead adjacent to the crimp. Tighten the wires.

6 Crimp the crimp bead (see Basics, p. 12). Trim the excess wire.
Open the loop on an earring wire and attach the earring. Close the loop. Make a second earring to match the first. ✤

SupplyList

- **20 or more** 4mm round crystals
- **1g** 11º seed beads
- **40 or more** 3–4mm flat spacers
- .010 or .012 flexible beading wire
- **2** crimp beads
- pair of earring wires
- chainnose pliers
- diagonal wire cutters
- crimping pliers (optional)

EDITOR'S TIP
Use .014 or .015 flexible beading wire for sturdier earrings. This works especially well for those larger in diameter.

Twisted-wire
jump rings and
smoky crystals
lend style and
sophistication
to a watch face

Keeping

1 To make the chain extender's dangle, string an 8mm crystal on a head pin. Make the first half of a wrapped loop (see Basics, p. 12) above the bead. Attach a 1-in. (2.5cm) chain and complete the wraps. Set aside.

2 Determine the finished length of your watchband. Divide that measurement in half, add 5 in. (13cm), and cut two pieces of beading wire to that length. On each wire, string a spacer, a crimp bead, and one loop of the watch face. Go back through the beads just strung and tighten the wires. Crimp the crimp beads (Basics) and trim the excess wire.

These days, watches aren't just functional, they're fashionable. The well-dressed woman owns more than one. With a mix of crystals and jingling jump rings, this watch will keep you on schedule with style. Whether you choose versatile clear crystals or a particular color, time will be on your side whenever you accessorize.

3 String an 8mm crystal and three twisted-wire jump rings on each wire. Repeat until the watchband is within 1 in. (2.5cm) of the desired length. End with a crystal on each side.

4 On one end, string a crimp bead, a spacer, and a lobster claw clasp. Go back through the last beads strung and tighten the wire. Repeat on the other end, substituting the chain extender for the clasp. Check the fit, and add or remove beads from each end if necessary. Crimp the crimp beads and trim the excess wire. ✤

EDITOR'S TIP
Try pairing square jump rings and cube crystals with a square watch face.

time

by Amy DeLeo and Lindsay O. Vance

Three crystal hues form a banded bracelet

Spectrum

Inspired by nature's palette (think golden meadows, ocean waves, fall harvest), three crystal colors blend for a beautiful bracelet. Choosing related hues unifies this bracelet, while the three-hole spacer bars divide the strands into distinct gradated sections. With three strands of 6mm crystals, this bracelet's natural beauty is a triple treat.

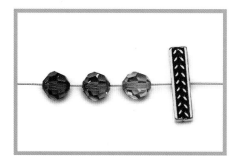

1 **a** Determine the finished length of your bracelet. Add 5 in. (13cm) and cut three pieces of beading wire to that length.

b On one wire, string a dark-colored crystal, a medium-colored crystal, a light-colored crystal, and the center hole of one spacer bar.

2 **a** Repeat the pattern in step 1b until the strand is within 2 in. (5cm) of the desired length, ending with a crystal.

b On each end, string a 3mm spacer, a crimp bead, a 2mm spacer, and the center loop of a three-to-one connector. Go back through the beads just strung. Do not crimp the crimp beads.

snapshot

by Anne Nikolai Kloss

3 **a** On the remaining wires, repeat steps 1b, 2a, and 2b, with the respective holes of the spacer and connector bars. Check the fit, and add or remove beads from each end if necessary. Crimp the crimp beads (see Basics, p. 12) and trim the excess wire.

b Open two jump rings (Basics) and attach each half of the clasp to the single loop on the connectors. Close the jump rings. ❖

Supply List

- **63 or more** 6mm round crystals, **21 or more** in each of three colors: dark, medium, and light
- **6 or more** 4 x 15mm three-hole spacer bars
- 2 4 x 15mm three-to-one connector bars
- 6 3mm round spacers
- 6 2mm round spacers
- flexible beading wire, .014 or .015
- 2 4mm jump rings
- 6 crimp beads
- toggle clasp
- 2 pairs of chainnose pliers
- diagonal wire cutters
- crimping pliers (optional)

EDITOR'S TIP
Before crimping, shape the bracelet into a circle and fasten the clasp. This will ensure flexibility so that the strands are not too tight.

TRIOS TO TRY

pinks
light: light rose
medium: rose champagne
dark: padparadscha

lighter reds
light: fire opal
medium: Indian red
dark: Siam

darker reds
light: Indian red
medium: Siam
dark: garnet

blue-greens
light: chrysolite
medium: erinite
dark: tourmaline

purples
light: violet AB
medium: tanzanite AB
dark: amethyst AB

blues
light: Indian sapphire
dark: Indian sapphire AB
medium: Pacific opal

yellow-greens
light: lime
medium: khaki
dark: olivine

browns
light: jonquil
medium: light Colorado topaz
dark: smoked topaz

Krystallos ladder

by **Rachel Nelson-Smith**

Create a cool cuff of crystals and pearls

The word "crystal" comes from the Greek "krystallos," meaning "ice." This cuff bracelet, however, is guaranteed to generate some fashion heat. Crystals and pearls create a free-form ladder that will bring you out of the cold and into the heights of style.

SupplyList

- **90–140** 4mm bicone crystals in two colors
- **6–12** 8mm or 12mm pearls
- 5 ft. (1.52m) 26-gauge half-hard wire
- 18 in. (46cm) 16-gauge dead-soft wire
- 6 in. (15cm) 24-gauge half-hard wire
- chainnose pliers
- roundnose pliers
- diagonal wire cutters

EDITOR'S TIP

Work with a length of wire that's comfortable. You can end a length and begin a new one by wrapping tightly several times at the top or bottom.

1 Find a round object approximately the desired diameter of your cuff. (A water bottle was used here.) Wrap an 18-in. (46cm) piece of 16-gauge wire around the object. Bend the wire down at a right angle with chainnose pliers, leaving a 1¼-in. (3.2cm) opening.

2 Make a right-angle bend about ¾ in. (1.9cm) from the first bend, and wrap the wire back around the object.
Bend the wire up at a right angle, keeping the 1¼-in. opening.
Make a right-angle bend about ¾ in. from the last bend. Leaving a ½-in. (1.3cm) overlap of the ends, trim the excess wire.

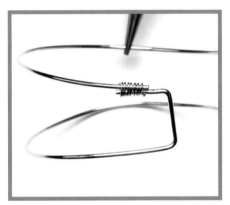

3 Cut a 3-in. (7.6cm) piece of 24-gauge wire. Tightly wrap the wire around the overlapping ends of the 16-gauge wire seven or eight times.

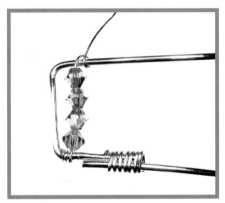

4 Tightly wrap the 26-gauge wire two or three times around the bottom 16-gauge wire at one end of the cuff. String three or four crystals in one color. Wrap the 26-gauge wire around the top wire several times and then around the bottom wire.

5 Continue stringing three or four crystals in alternating colors for five columns, then string one or two pearls. Repeat this pattern to the end of the cuff.

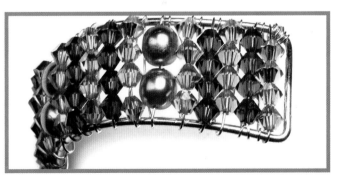

6 Wrap the 26-gauge wire two or three times around the 16-gauge wire, and trim the excess. ❖

The designer offers kits for this project. See p. 255 for contact information.

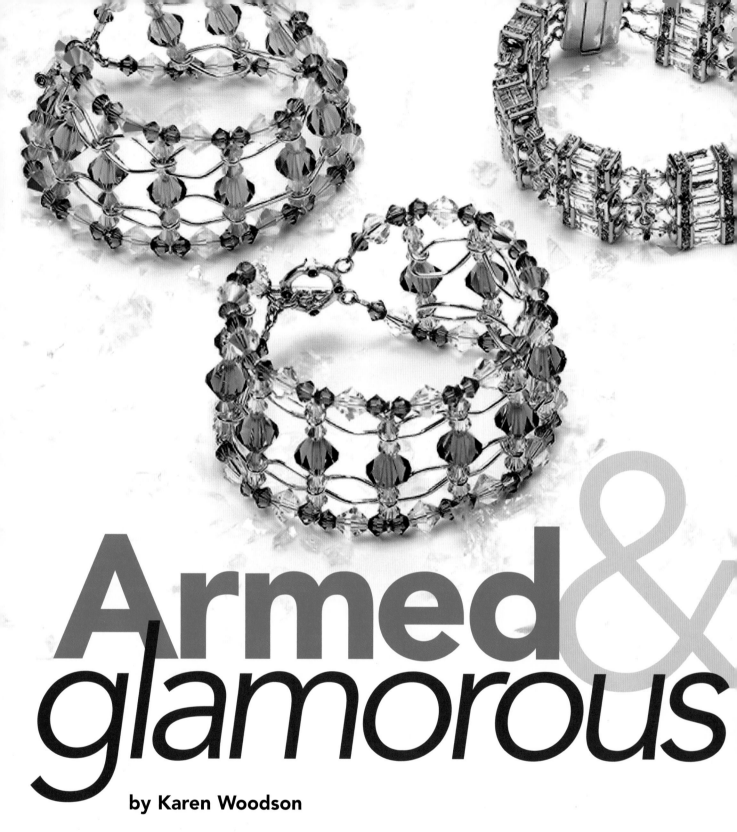

Armed&
glamorous

by Karen Woodson

Arm yourself with three new looks created with tried-and-true crystal and chain elements. Squaredelles give substance to lightweight cube crystals in elegant, but distinctly different, styles, and cleverly woven eye pins join two lengths of diamond chain for a lovely ladder effect. The right to bare arms was never more stylish.

A trio of crystal bracelets creates new options for classic materials

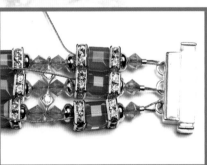

1a **triple-strand cuff** • Determine the finished length of your bracelet. Add 5 in. (13cm) and cut three strands of beading wire to that length.

b On the top and bottom wires, center a gold squaredelle, a cube crystal, and a gold squaredelle. On the middle wire, center a silver squaredelle, a cube crystal, and a silver squaredelle.

2a On the top and bottom wires, string a gold spacer and a bicone crystal. String a silver spacer and a bicone on the middle wire. String a three-hole spacer bar on the corresponding wires. String a bicone and a gold spacer on the top and bottom wires, and a bicone and a silver spacer on the middle wire.

b Repeat the patterns in steps 1b and 2a until the strands are within 1½ in. (3.8cm) of the desired length. End with the pattern from step 1b.

3 On each end, string a spacer, a bicone, a crimp bead, and the corresponding loop of half of the clasp. Go back through the beads just strung and tighten the wires. Check the fit, and add or remove beads if necessary. Crimp the crimp beads (see Basics, p. 12), and trim the excess wire.

Design Guidelines

• The toggle clasp used with both the chain and woven squaredelle cuffs was made with a two-jump-ring ending on the bar half of the clasp. If using a toggle clasp with a single-jump-ring ending, either attach both strands to the single jump ring, or add two jump rings to the bar before attaching the strands.

• Use a double-strand clasp and spacer bars for a narrower version of the triple-strand cuff. Use gold findings on one strand and silver on the other, or select just one for a monochromatic look.

1 **a** chain cuff • Determine the finished length of your bracelet. Add 5 in. (13cm) and cut two strands of beading wire to that length. Cut two lengths of chain 2 in. (5cm) shorter than the desired length of your bracelet. (These are 5 in., or 10 large links and 11 small links.)

b On a 2-in. eye pin, string: color B 4mm bicone crystal, the first small link of one chain, B 4mm bicone, color A 8mm bicone, B 4mm bicone, the first small link of the second chain, B 4mm bicone. Make a plain loop (Basics) next to the bicone.

2 Repeat step 1b for the remaining small links.

3 String a color A 4mm bicone, a color B 6mm bicone, and an A 4mm bicone on the beading wire. String the top loop of the first eye pin unit. Repeat until you have strung all of the top eye pin loops. End with a crystal pattern. Repeat with the bottom eye pin loops.

4 On each end, string a crimp bead and the corresponding loop of half of the clasp. Go back through the beads just strung and tighten the wires. Check the fit, and add or remove beads or chain if necessary. Crimp the crimp beads, and trim the excess wire.

SupplyList

The following materials will make 7-in. (18cm) bracelets.

all projects
- flexible beading wire, .014 or .015
- chainnose or crimping pliers
- diagonal wire cutters

triple-strand cuff
- **21** 6mm cube crystals
- **42** 4mm bicone crystals
- **28** 6mm gold squaredelles
- **14** 6mm silver squaredelles
- **28** 6mm gold saucer spacers

- **14** 6mm silver saucer spacers
- **6** three-strand cubic zirconia spacer bars (Too Cute Beads, 866-342-3237, toocutebeads.com)
- **6** crimp beads
- three-strand push clasp (Too Cute Beads)

chain cuff
- **11** 8mm bicone crystals, color A
- **92** 4mm bicone crystals in two colors, 48 color A, 44 color B
- **24** 6mm bicone crystals, color B
- **1** ft. (30cm) chain, diamond-shaped links (Too Cute Beads)
- **11** 2-in. (5cm) eye pins

- **4** crimp beads
- two-strand crystal toggle clasp (Too Cute Beads)
- roundnose pliers

woven squaredelle cuff
- **15** 6mm cube crystals
- **30** 6mm saucer crystals (Shipwreck Beads, 800-950-4232, shipwreckbeads.com)
- **30** 6mm silver squaredelles
- **64** 4mm bicone crystals
- **32** 3mm round silver spacers
- **4** crimp beads
- two-strand crystal toggle clasp (Too Cute Beads)

1a woven squaredelle cuff
Determine the finished length of your bracelet, triple the measurement, add 5 in., and cut two strands of beading wire to that length.

b Over both wires, string: saucer crystal, squaredelle, cube crystal, squaredelle, saucer. Center the beads.

c On each end of each wire, string a bicone crystal, a spacer, and a bicone.

2a On one end of one wire, string: saucer, squaredelle, cube, squaredelle, saucer. String the other end of that wire through the pattern from the opposite direction, keeping the tension on the wires as even as possible. Repeat on the other side.

b Repeat steps 1c and 2a until the bracelet is within 1½ in. (3.8cm) of the desired length. End with step 1c.

3 On each strand on one side, string a crimp bead and one loop of half of the clasp. Go back through the last four beads strung and tighten the wires. Repeat on the other side. Check the fit, and add or remove beads if necessary. Crimp the crimp beads, and trim the excess wire. ❖

Delicate

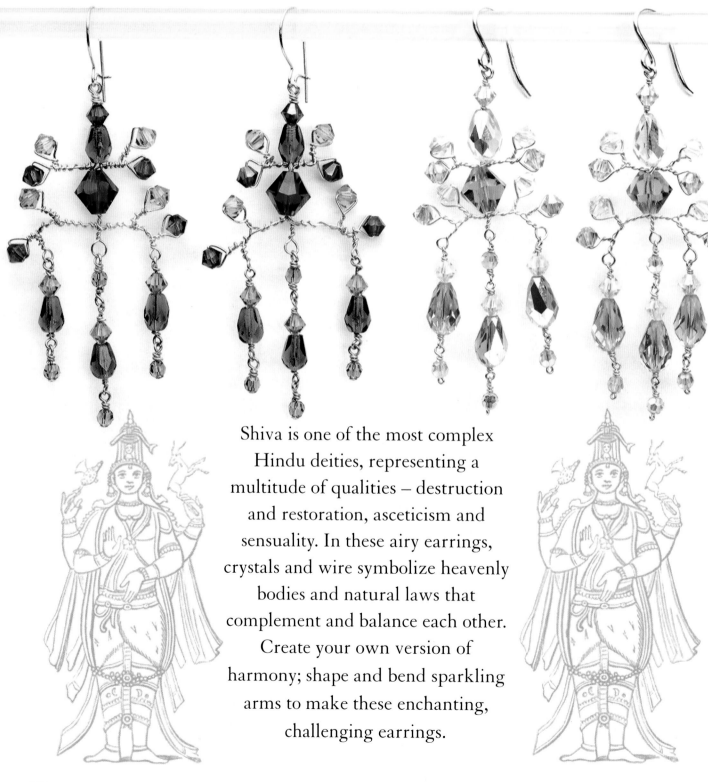

Shiva is one of the most complex Hindu deities, representing a multitude of qualities – destruction and restoration, asceticism and sensuality. In these airy earrings, crystals and wire symbolize heavenly bodies and natural laws that complement and balance each other. Create your own version of harmony; shape and bend sparkling arms to make these enchanting, challenging earrings.

balance

Suspend crystals in airy earrings • **by Rachel Nelson-Smith**

1 String a 3mm round crystal on a head pin. Make a wrapped loop (see Basics, p. 12) above the crystal. Cut a 2½-in. (6.4cm) piece of wire. Make the first half of a wrapped loop at one end. Attach the crystal dangle and complete the wraps.

2 String a crystal drop and a color A 4mm bicone crystal. Make a wrapped loop above the top bicone. Repeat steps 1 and 2 to make a total of three drop units. Set two drop units aside for step 5.

3 Cut a 2-in. (5cm) piece of wire. Make the first half of a wrapped loop at one end. Attach a drop unit and complete the wraps. String a round crystal and make a wrapped loop.

4 Cut an 18-in. (46cm) piece of wire. Make the first half of a wrapped loop at the center. Attach the longest drop unit, and twist the wires several times.

5 On each side, approximately ½ in. (1.3cm) from the center loop, make the first half of a wrapped loop. Attach a drop unit to each loop, and twist the wires together several times.

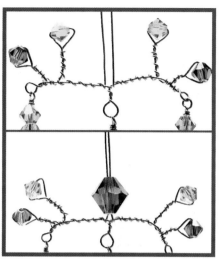

6 On each side, approximately ¼ in. (6mm) from the last twist, string a color B 4mm bicone crystal. Bend the wire around the bicone, and twist the wires together several times.

7 Repeat step 6, substituting an A 4mm bicone for the B 4mm bicone. Twist the wires until they meet above the center drop unit.

String an 8mm bicone crystal over both wires.

8 On each side, approximately ¼ in. from the 8mm bicone, string a B bicone. Bend the wire around the bicone, and twist the wires together several times.

Approximately ¼ in. from the last twist, repeat, substituting an A bicone for the B bicone. Twist the wires until they meet above the 8mm bicone.

9 String a crystal drop and a B bicone. Make a wrapped loop above the bicone with both wires.

10 Attach the dangle on the loop of a kidney earring wire. If using a French earring wire, open the loop and attach the dangle. Close the loop. Make a second earring to match the first. ❖

The designer offers kits for this project. See p. 255 for contact information.

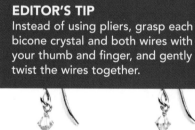

EDITOR'S TIP
Instead of using pliers, grasp each bicone crystal and both wires with your thumb and finger, and gently twist the wires together.

Shortcuts

Readers' tips to make your beading life easier

1 storing necklaces...
For an inexpensive and attractive display option that can hold many necklaces, find a hand-towel bar at a discount bath store. A variety of sizes and styles is available, including some with bars of graduated heights.
– *Viki Gayhardt, Deerfield, N.H.*

2 ...and bracelets
Mug trees from housewares stores are great for storing bracelets or short necklaces. They are available in different finishes to match your bedroom decor. With eight pegs, you can store more than 65 bracelets.
– *Amanda Bohm, Austin, Texas, and Christine Maree, South Africa*

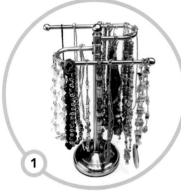

3 straightening fishing line
To uncurl fishing line, place it in hot water or over steam for a moment. The fishing line will relax and will be ready for your project in a few seconds.
– *Cynthia Poh, via e-mail*

4 consistent finishing
After looping beading wire back through a crimp bead, insert one jaw of your roundnose pliers into the loop and pull the wire taut. This balances the tension and helps you create the same size loop each time.
– *Tammy Powley, via e-mail*

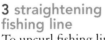

5 closing crimp covers
Use the first notch in your crimping pliers to close crimp covers. The rounded notch closes the cover completely while preserving its shape.
– *Paulette Biedenbender, Franklin, Wis.*

6 revolving display
To display many earrings, hang them in the holes of an inverted mesh trash can. Place the trash can on a lazy Susan to see your jewelry at a glance.
– *Catie Hoover, via e-mail*

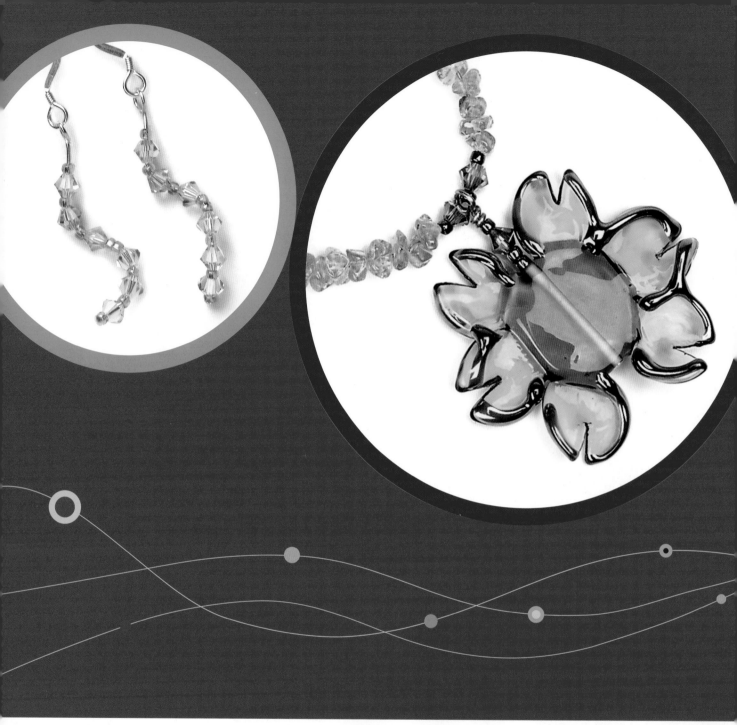

Mixed

materials

Lush
and

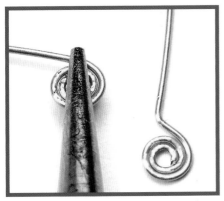

1 **necklace** • To make a wire spiral for a front-to-back–drilled bead, cut a 3-in. (7.6cm) piece of wire. Grasp the end of the wire with the tip of your roundnose pliers and form a small loop. After a complete turn, gently grasp the wire with chainnose pliers. Continue to form a spiral with your fingers until you have two or three coils.

2 String a crystal on the wire. Using the tip of your roundnose pliers, form a zig-zag pattern approximately ¼ in. (6.4mm) above the crystal. Bend the top of the wire up.

3 Using the largest part of your roundnose pliers, make the first half of a wrapped loop (see Basics, p. 12) perpendicular to the spiral, approximately ½ in. (1.3cm) above the last zig-zag.

leafy lariat

by Jane Konkel

Glass and plastic merge along a line of copper

Mix multicolored glass beads with plastic leaf-shaped beads for a splendid spin on today's trinket trend. Copper chain is the stalk's trellis, while wire veins and tendrils embellish each leaf. Combine unexpected colors inspired by ever-changing foliage for an autumnal necklace and earrings set.

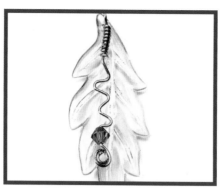

4 String a leaf bead on the loop and complete the wraps.
Repeat steps 1–4 for the remaining front-to-back–drilled beads.

5 To make a wire spiral for a side-to-side–drilled bead, follow step 1. Bend the top of the wire up. String a crystal on the wire.
Place the largest part of your roundnose pliers approximately 1½ in. (3.8cm) from the end of the wire. Make the first half of a wrapped loop parallel to the spiral.

6 String a leaf bead on the wire and complete the wraps.
Repeat steps 5 and 6 for the remaining side-to-side–drilled beads.

7 Determine the finished length of the lariat's choker. (This choker is 15 in./38cm.) Double the measurement and cut a piece of chain to that length. Open a jump ring (Basics) and attach both ends of chain and the toggle half of the clasp. Close the jump ring. Attach another jump ring, the doubled chain's center link, and the bar half of the clasp.

8 Determine the finished length of your lariat's dangle. (This dangle is 7 in./18cm.) Cut a piece of chain to that length. Open a jump ring. Attach a leaf unit to one end of the chain. Close the jump ring. Continue attaching leaf units to the chain with jump rings, skipping one to seven links between units.

9 Open a jump ring. Attach the remaining end of the chain to the toggle clasp. Close the jump ring. Check the fit, and trim links from the ends if necessary.

Supply List

necklace
- **10–15** glass or plastic leaf-shaped beads
- **10–15** 4mm bicone crystals
- 45 in. (1m) 20- or 22-gauge copper wire, or a combination of gauges
- 35–40 in. (.9–1m) copper curb chain (Rings & Things, 800-366-2156, rings-things.com)
- **13–18** 4mm copper jump rings
- copper toggle clasp (Rings & Things)
- chainnose pliers
- roundnose pliers
- diagonal wire cutters

earrings
- **4** glass or plastic leaf-shaped beads
- **4** 4mm bicone crystals
- 12 in. (30cm) 20- or 22-gauge copper wire, or a combination of gauges
- 3 in. (7.6cm) copper curb chain (Rings & Things)
- **4** 4mm copper jump rings
- pair of niobium earring wires (Fire Mountain Gems, 800-355-2137, firemountaingems.com)
- chainnose pliers
- roundnose pliers
- diagonal wire cutters

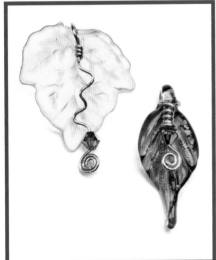

1 earrings • Make a wire spiral for two leaf-shaped beads. To make a wire spiral for a front-to-back–drilled bead, follow steps 1–4 of the necklace. To make a wire spiral for a side-to-side–drilled bead, follow steps 1, 5, and 6 of the necklace.

2 Cut a 1½-in. piece of chain. Open two jump rings and attach a leaf unit to each end of the chain. Close the jump rings.

3 Open the loop on an earring wire and attach the dangle. Close the loop. Make a second earring to match the first. ❖

An art bead blossoms on a silk cord necklace • by Irina Miech

Lily original

Seed beads will sprout into something spectacular when integrated with crystals, dyed silk cord, and a fabulous calla lily art bead. Because silk cords come in a multitude of intense colors, the possible combinations seem endless. So, your necklace, just like a lily found in nature, will be one of a kind.

1 String a bicone crystal on a head pin. Make the first half of a wrapped loop (see Basics, p. 12) above the crystal. Make a total of four bicone units. Set one unit aside for the extender in step 10.

2 **a** Cut a ½-in. (1.3cm) piece of 2mm chain. Cut two more pieces, each ¼ in. (6mm) longer than the previous piece. Attach a bicone unit's loop to each chain and complete the wraps.
b Cut three 4-in. (10cm) pieces of 22-gauge wire. Make the first half of a wrapped loop on one end of each wire. Complete the wraps on two wires and set aside for step 7. On the remaining wire, attach the chain dangles and complete the wraps.

3 String a crystal rondelle, the art bead, and a rondelle on the wire. Make a wrapped loop above the rondelle.

4 Determine the finished length of your necklace. (These are 15 in./38cm.) Add 6 in. (15cm) and cut a piece of beading wire and two pieces of silk cord to that length. Center the pendant on the wire and silk cords.

EDITOR'S TIP
Depending on the size of the art bead, you may need to turn the 8mm crystal rondelle sideways in order to fit it in the top of the flower. If so, string the wire through the rondelle after it's inside the art bead.

SupplyList

- 60mm art bead (by Greg Hoff, at Eclectica, 262-641-0910)
- **8** 8mm crystal rondelles
- **22–26** 5mm bicone crystals
- 1g 11º seed beads
- flexible beading wire, .014 or .015
- 12 in. (30cm) 22-gauge half-hard wire
- 2½ in. (6.4cm) chain, 2mm links
- 2½ in. (6.4cm) chain, 5mm links
- **4** 1½-in. (3.8cm) head pins
- **2** crimp beads
- **2** 24mm beading cones
- S-hook clasp
- **2** 18–22 in. (46–56cm) silk cords, in 2 colors (Eclectica)
- chainnose pliers
- roundnose pliers
- diagonal wire cutters
- crimping pliers (optional)

5 On each end of the wire, string: bicone, rondelle, bicone, 13–16 11º seed beads. Repeat this pattern two more times.

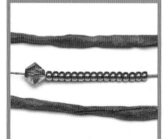

6 On each end of the wire, string a bicone and 13–16 11ºs. Repeat this pattern until the necklace is within 2 in. (5cm) of the desired length.

7 On each end of the beading wire, string a crimp bead, an 11º, and the wrapped loop of the wire from step 2b. Go back through the last three beads and tighten the wire. Check the fit, and add or remove an equal number of beads from each end if necessary. Crimp the crimp beads (Basics). String both ends of silk cord through the wrapped loop.

8 Make two overhand knots in the ends of the silk cord (Basics). On each end, string a beading cone and a bicone.

9 On one end, make a wrapped loop above the bicone. Attach the S-hook clasp to the loop.

10 On the other end, make the first half of a wrapped loop above the bicone. Attach the 5mm chain and complete the wraps. Attach the bicone unit from step 1 to the chain and complete the wraps. ❖

TEXTILE STYLE

Weave rag yarn
around beads in a
fashion-forward necklace

by Brenda Schweder

When fashion emphasizes fabric textures (velvet, suede, and vintage denim and brocade), jewelry follows suit. Beads combine with textiles for a multimedia necklace: Frayed yarn edges hug the beads' curves, balancing the raw and the refined. Create your one-of-a-kind piece with cotton rag yarn and beads in a range of colors and textures. Knot the necklace to collar length, or wear it longer to show more yarn. Both organic and orderly, this necklace will appeal to your trendsetting personality.

1 Determine the finished length of your necklace. (These are 39 in./1m.) Add 15 in. (38cm) and cut a piece of rag yarn to that length. Determine the finished length of the beaded section. (The beaded sections of these are 16 in./41cm.) Add 8 in. (20cm) and cut a piece of beading wire to that length. String a crimp bead on the beading wire, and make a loop around the yarn approximately 12 in. (30cm) from one end. Go through the crimp bead, tighten the wire, and crimp the crimp bead (see Basics, p. 12). Trim the excess wire to ⅛ in. (3mm).

2 Tie an overhand knot (Basics) with the yarn, hiding the crimp bead in the knot. Make sure the working end of the wire faces the same direction as the working part of the yarn.

EDITOR'S TIP
To make needle threading easier, flatten the tip of the beading wire with chainnose pliers first. Though any sewing needle with an eye large enough for the wire will work, a tapestry needle (size 24) makes threading easy.

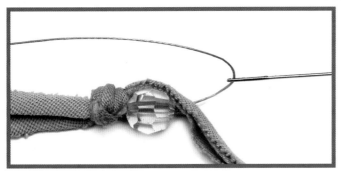

3 Thread the wire through a needle, leaving a 4-in. (10cm) tail. String the wire through a bead and the yarn. The yarn should cover half of the bead. For a more refined appearance, fold the yarn lengthwise before stringing.

4 Continue stringing beads and going through the yarn, looping the yarn in alternating directions around each bead. When the beaded section is the desired length, bring the wire through the yarn and remove the needle.

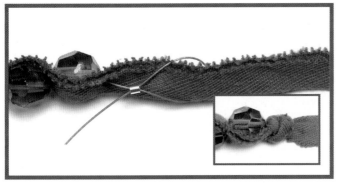

5 String a crimp bead. Loop the wire around the yarn and go back through the crimp bead. Tighten the wire, and crimp the crimp bead. Trim the excess wire to 1/8 in. Tie an overhand knot with the yarn, hiding the crimp bead in the knot. Check the fit, and trim the yarn ends if necessary.

6 If desired, string a bead 1¼ in. (3.2cm) from each end, and tie an overhand knot next to the bead. If you have trouble stringing the yarn, trim it lengthwise, or use a needle to push it through the bead. ❖

Design Guidelines

Look for beads in gradated colors or unusual textures, and make sure the holes are large enough to accommodate a needle. Some of our favorites:

1. NATURALS Try wood, bone, or seeds with unbleached yarn.

2. LUCITE Use candy colors that complement the hues in your yarn.

3. METAL Laser-cut and Bali-silver beads shine in a multitude of textures.

The designer offers kits for this project. See p. 255 for contact information.

Supply List

- **40–70** 7–12mm large-hole round beads
- 4½–5½ ft. (1.4–1.7m) R2 rag yarn (Ruhama's, 414-332-2660, ruhamas.com)
- flexible beading wire, .014 or .015
- 2 crimp beads
- chainnose or crimping pliers
- diagonal wire cutters
- sewing needle to accommodate flexible beading wire
- scissors

Strike a
CORD

Use silk beading cord to string an easy, convertible necklace

by Florence Sauerbrey

Forgo the flexible beading wire and create a casual necklace using silk cord and leftover beads. There are no set rules for this necklace, so take advantage of its versatility and make it to suit your taste. You can play it safe with a consistent pattern or take an asymmetrical approach by stringing beads randomly. Wear it long and loosely tied as a lariat, or wrap it around to wear it choker length.

1 Tie an overhand knot (see Basics, p. 12) at one end of the beading cord. String six to ten gemstones and crystals, and tie an overhand knot next to the last bead strung.

2 Tie an overhand knot 2–3 in. (5–7.6cm) from the previous knot. String three to seven gemstones, pearls, or crystals. Tie an overhand knot.

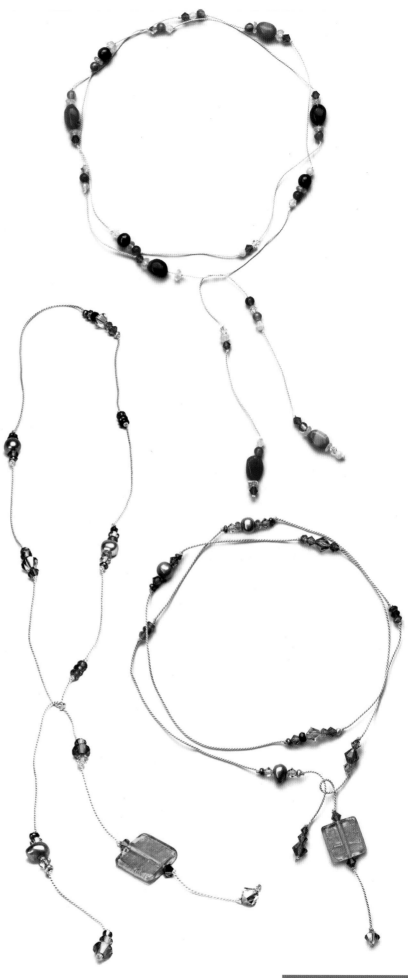

3 Repeat step 2 until the strand is within 3–4 in. (7.6–10cm) of the desired length. Tie a knot 2–3 in. (5–7.6cm) from the previous knot. String six to ten gemstones and crystals, and tie an overhand knot. Trim the excess cord from both ends and apply glue to the end knots. ✤

SUPPLY NOTE
Griffin silk cord comes in a variety of colors and has an attached needle that is great for stringing small-hole beads such as pearls.

SupplyList

- **15–50** gemstones, assorted shapes and sizes
- **20–35** bicone crystals, assorted sizes
- **2–6** pearls, assorted shapes and sizes
- card of silk beading cord, size 4 or 5
- G-S Hypo Cement

FIT to be TIED

Combine
beads, wire,
and leather in
an easy lariat

by Ronna Sarvas Weltman

In place of knots, wirework spirals add a geometric touch to each end of this leather lariat. For extra details, oxidize the wire first, then run it through a polishing cloth to create dimension. Loop your lariat 'round your neck to complete your casual style.

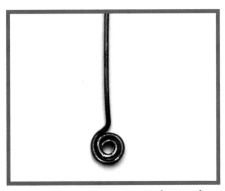

1 Cut a 4-in. (10cm) piece of wire. If desired, oxidize the wire with Midas Black Max or liver of sulfur according to the manufacturer's instructions. Grasp the end of the wire with the tip of your roundnose pliers and form a small loop. After a complete turn, hold the wire in place with chainnose pliers. Continue to make coils with your fingers until you have formed a spiral.

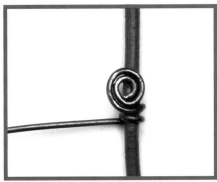

2 a Wrap the leather cord around your neck, add 6 in. (15cm), and trim it to that length. (The brown lariat is 19 in./48cm; the green lariat, 23 in./58cm.)

 b Tightly wrap the spiral's wire around the cord ¼ in. (6mm) from one end. Make one or two more wraps, ending with the remaining wire on the opposite side of the spiral.

3 With the remaining wire, make a spiral or other decorative design. To make a triangular design, bend the wire with chainnose pliers. Repeat step 1, if desired, to make additional spirals or decorative designs.

4 String two rondelles and an accent bead. Tie an overhand knot (see Basics, p. 12) above the beads.

5 On the other end, string an accent bead and two rondelles. Repeat steps 1, 2b, and 3. Tie an overhand knot above the beads. ❖

Supply List

- 2 large-hole accent beads, approximately 10 x 14mm
- 4 7–9mm large-hole rondelles
- 20–30 in. (51–76cm) leather cord, 1.5mm diameter
- 8–16 in. (20–41cm) 22- or 24-gauge half-hard sterling silver wire
- chainnose pliers
- roundnose pliers
- diagonal wire cutters
- Midas Black Max or liver of sulfur solution

EDITOR'S TIP
To touch up oxidized wire after it's attached to the leather, use a cotton swab dipped in the blackening solution.

BOULDER
statement

Given their sedimentary lifestyle and rocky start, who could have predicted that Stone-agers Wilma Flintstone and Betty Rubble would one day become fashion icons? Lightweight resin rocks, suspended from suede and accented with silver, are an easy transition into the big-bead trend. Make Wilma and Betty proud: Make a boulder statement.

1 Cut a 14-in. (36cm) piece of beading wire. String an alternating pattern of three dark-colored nuggets and accent beads. String an accent bead on each end. Center the beads on the wire.

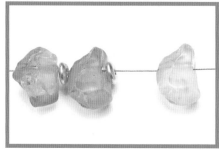

2 On each end, string: medium-colored nugget, accent bead, medium-colored nugget, accent bead, light-colored nugget.

Create a landslide

of gradated colors on

a suede cord for an

earthy necklace

by Jane Konkel

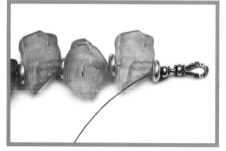

3 On each end, string: accent bead, 5mm spacer, crimp bead, 5mm spacer, ten 2mm square spacers. Go back through the 5mm spacer, the crimp bead, the 5mm spacer, and the accent bead. Tighten the wires. Crimp the crimp beads (see Basics, p. 12) and trim the excess wire.

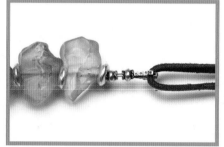

4 Determine the finished length of each of the suede parts of your necklace. (These are 6 in./15cm.) Double that measurement and cut two pieces of suede cord to that length. Center each beaded loop on each of the cords. Fold each cord in half.

5 On each side, attach a connector to the doubled cord approximately ½ in. (1.3cm) from the fold. Using chainnose pliers, crimp the connector.

Check the length, allowing 2 in. (5cm) for finishing. Trim an equal amount from each end, if necessary.

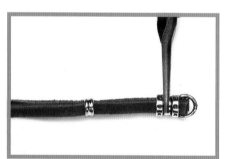

6 **a** Attach a connector approximately ¾ in. (1.9cm) from the ends of the cord.

b String one pair of cords through a 4mm crimp end. Using chainnose pliers, flatten the center (crimp portion) of the crimp end. Repeat on the other side.

7 Open a jump ring (Basics) and attach the loop to half of the hook-and-eye clasp. Close the jump ring. Repeat on the other side. ❖

EDITOR'S TIP
If you prefer the look of a round (rather than flat) cord, try waxed leather cord.

Supply List

- strand resin nuggets (The Bead Goes On, 866-861-2323, beadgoeson.com)
- **10** 10mm silver accent beads
- **4** 5mm spacers
- **20** 2mm square spacers
- flexible beading wire, .018 or .019
- **2** crimp beads
- **4** connectors (large crimps for cord, Rio Grande, 800-545-6566)
- **2** 4mm crimp ends with loops
- hook-and-eye clasp with **2** 5mm jump rings
- 14–24 in. (36–61cm) suede cord, 3mm width
- **2** pairs of chainnose pliers
- diagonal wire cutters
- crimping pliers (optional)

Perfect touch

Bold beads showcase a substantial pendant • **by Rupa Balachandar**

Texture can add interest to the simplest of necklaces, especially when craggy natural and carved materials, like wood and seeds, are mixed with a smooth, glossy pendant. Let your fingers do the talking when you choose the elements for this tactile creation.

1 Determine the finished length of your necklace. (These are 17 in./ 43cm.) Add 6 in. (15cm) and cut a piece of beading wire to that length. Center the pendant on the wire and string three 6º seed beads. The pendant loop will rest on these beads when the necklace is finished.

2 On each side of the pendant, string a textured bead and a spacer. Repeat this pattern until the necklace is within 2 in. (5cm) of the desired length.

3 On one end, string: crimp bead, five 8ºs, a 6º, and half of the toggle clasp. Go back through the last beads strung and tighten the wire. Repeat on the other end. Check the fit, and add or remove an equal number of beads from each end if necessary. Crimp the crimp beads (see Basics, p. 12) and trim the excess wire. ❖

EDITOR'S TIP
Use a toggle clasp that's substantial enough to support the weight of the materials you choose.

SupplyList

- 30–40mm pendant in silver setting
- 18-in. (46cm) strand textured beads
- **5** 6º seed beads
- **10** 8º seed beads
- **20–34** 4–5mm silver disk spacers
- flexible beading wire, .014 or .015
- **2** crimp beads
- toggle clasp
- chainnose or crimping pliers
- diagonal wire cutters

NATIVE CHARMS

Suspend a carved pendant and charms from a gold-chain necklace

by Brenda Schweder

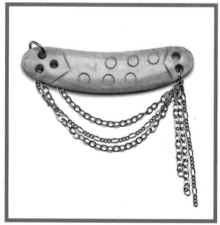

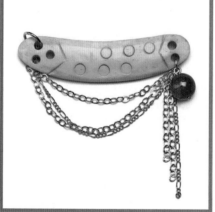

1 necklace • Cut two 6-in. (15cm) pieces of cable chain and a 6-in. piece of figaro chain. Open an 8mm jump ring (see Basics, p. 12). Attach the three chains and the top hole of one side of the pendant. Close the jump ring. Open a 6mm jump ring and attach the bottom hole of the other side of the pendant. Attach the jump ring to a link of each chain so the chains drape at various lengths.

2 String a round bead on a head pin. Make a plain loop (Basics) above the bead.

Open the loop and attach the dangle to the 6mm jump ring on the pendant. Close the loop.

3 To make a tassel, cut a 42-in. (1.1m) piece of cord. Wrap it around three of your fingers ten times. Remove the cord. Cut a 6-in. piece of cord and tie a surgeon's knot (Basics) around the top of the loop.

EDITOR'S TIP
A longer version of this necklace is also a stylish option. To hang the pendant, substitute cable chain with 5mm links. You'll need 26 in. (66cm) or more of the larger cable chain.

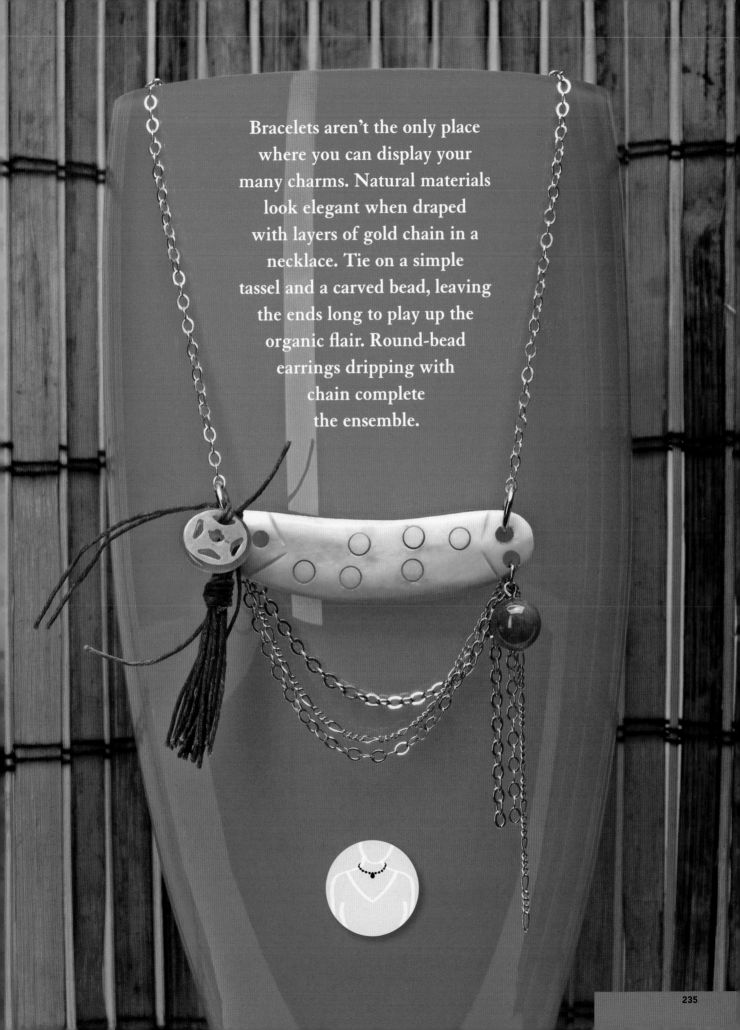

Bracelets aren't the only place where you can display your many charms. Natural materials look elegant when draped with layers of gold chain in a necklace. Tie on a simple tassel and a carved bead, leaving the ends long to play up the organic flair. Round-bead earrings dripping with chain complete the ensemble.

4 Cut a 12-in. (30cm) piece of cord. Wrap it around the bundle of cords several times, ¼ in. (6mm) below the knot. Tie a surgeon's knot and trim the excess cord. Cut the bottom part of the loop to open the tassel.

5 Tie a surgeon's knot around the 8mm jump ring with the tassel's top cord. Trim the excess cord to the desired length.

Cut a 3-in. (7.6cm) piece of cord. Fold it in half and string a disk bead and the 8mm jump ring over both ends. Go through the cord's loop. Tighten the ends and apply glue to the knot. Trim the excess cord, leaving the ends 1½ in. (3.8cm) long.

6 Determine the finished length of your necklace. (This one is 15 in./38cm.) Subtract 2 in. (5cm), divide that number in half, and cut two pieces of cable chain to that length. Attach one chain to the 8mm jump ring. Open another 8mm jump ring and attach the remaining chain to the other side of the pendant.

7 Check the fit. Allow 1 in. (2.5cm) for the finishing, and trim the chain on each end if necessary. On one end, attach the lobster claw clasp with a 4mm jump ring. Repeat on the other end, substituting a soldered jump ring for the clasp.

1 earrings • Cut a 2½-in. (6.4cm) piece of wire. Make a plain loop at one end. String a round bead and make a wrapped loop (Basics) above the bead.

2 Open the loop of an earring wire and attach the wrapped loop. Close the earring wire's loop.

3 Cut a 3-in. and a 3½-in. (8.9cm) piece of cable chain. Cut a 3¼-in. (8.3cm) piece of figaro chain. Fold each chain in half. Open the dangle's loop and attach the center link of each chain. Close the loop. Make a second earring to match the first. ❧

The designer offers kits for these projects. See p. 255 for contact information.

See p. 255 for contact information.

SupplyList

necklace
- 15 x 60mm bone pendant (Beads and Pieces, beadsandpieces.com)
- 13mm disk bead
- 9mm round bead
- 25–32 in. (64–81cm) cable chain, 3mm links
- 6 in. (15cm) figaro chain, 2–3mm links
- 63 in. (1.6m) waxed cotton or linen cord, 1mm diameter
- 1½-in. (3.8cm) head pin
- 2 8mm jump rings
- 6mm jump ring
- 2 4mm jump rings
- lobster claw clasp and soldered jump ring
- chainnose pliers
- roundnose pliers
- diagonal wire cutters
- E6000 adhesive

earrings
- 2 9mm round beads
- 5 in. (13cm) 20-gauge half-hard wire
- 14 in. (36cm) cable chain, 3mm links
- 7 in. (18cm) figaro chain, 2–3mm links
- pair of earring wires
- chainnose pliers
- roundnose pliers
- diagonal wire cutters

Reel in a catch

Knot shells on cord for a distinctive bangle bracelet and earrings

by Brenda Schweder

Shell out for seaside treasures without spending a fortune. Waxed linen cord traps beads on a wood bangle, and earrings accent the organic theme. Your own catch of the day is sure to be fresh.

1 bracelet • Cut an 8-ft. (2.4m) piece of waxed linen cord. Tie a surgeon's knot (see Basics, p. 12) around the bangle, leaving a 3-in. (7.6cm) tail.

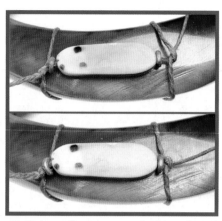

2 String a flat spacer, a shell bead, and a spacer. Pulling the cord taut, wrap it around the bangle and tie a knot flush with the spacer.

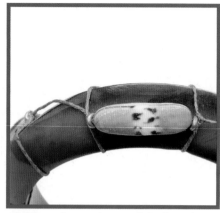

3 Wrap the cord around the bangle, and knot it against the bangle's next beveled edge. Repeat step 2. Continue around the entire bangle.

4 String a tube-shaped bead. Pull the cord taut, and tie a knot around the first knot you made.

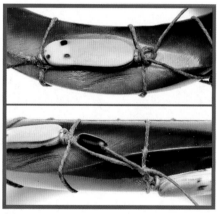

5 a String the cord under the adjacent shell, and tie a knot around the adjacent knot.
  b String a tube and tie a knot around the existing knot. Repeat until you reach the cord's tail from step 1.

6 Tie the ends together with a surgeon's knot. Glue the knot, and trim the excess cord to ⅛ in. (3mm). Tuck the knot under the shell.

Supply List

bracelet
- wood bangle bracelet with beveled edges
- **6–12** 8 x 25mm shell beads
- **6–12** 4 x 8mm tube-shaped beads
- **12–24** 4mm flat spacers
- 8 ft. (2.4m) 4-ply waxed linen cord, 1mm diameter
- G-S Hypo Cement

earrings
- **2** 8 x 25mm shell beads
- **4** 4 x 8mm tube-shaped beads
- **10** 4mm flat spacers
- 20 in. (51cm) 4-ply waxed linen cord, 1mm diameter
- pair of lever-back earring wires
- chainnose pliers
- G-S Hypo Cement

EDITOR'S TIP
Before stringing, cut the waxed linen cord at an angle.
The slanted tip will pass through the beads more easily.

1 earrings • Cut a 10-in. (25cm) piece of waxed linen cord. Fold it in half. Leaving a small loop, tie an overhand knot (Basics) with both ends.

2 On one end, string three flat spacers and a tube-shaped bead. Approximately 1 in. (2.5cm) from the loop's knot, tie an overhand knot. String two spacers and a tube. Tie an overhand knot ¾ in. (1.9cm) from the previous knot.

3 On the other end, string a shell bead. Tie an overhand knot 1½ in. (3.8cm) from the loop's knot. Trim the cord ends as desired.

4 Open the loop of an earring wire. Attach the dangle and close the loop. Make a second earring to match the first. ❖

The designer offers kits for these projects. See p. 255 for contact information.

Art exhibit

Memory wire and rubber tubing provide a great canvas for art beads • by Jean Yates

Using memory wire is so effortless, it's amazing how beautiful the final result can be. Grab those art beads that you just had to have – but haven't figured out how to showcase – and display them on a worthy framework.

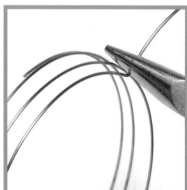

1 Separate four coils of memory wire from the stack of coils. Hold the wire with chainnose pliers and bend it back and forth at one place until the wire breaks. You also can use heavy-duty wire cutters. Do not use jewelry-weight wire cutters.

2 Using roundnose pliers, make a small loop on one end of the memory wire.

3 String a round crystal, an 8mm bead, a bicone crystal, and 2 in. (5cm) of rubber tubing.

SUPPLY NOTES

The polymer clay beads used in two of these bracelets are made by Emma Ralph, ejrbeads.co.uk. The pewter charms on those bracelets are from Green Girl Studios, greengirlstudios.com. The carved wooden beads are available at Eclectica, (262) 641-0910; leaf charms are available from Fire Mountain Gems, (800) 355-2137, or firemountaingems.com.

4 String: art bead, round, 8mm, bicone, 1½ in. (3.8cm) of tubing. Repeat this pattern four more times.

5 String a bicone, an 8mm, and a round. Cut the memory wire ¼ in. (6mm) from the last bead. Make a small loop on the end of the wire.

6 Open a jump ring (see Basics, p. 12) and string a charm, a 6º seed bead, and another charm. Attach the jump ring to a loop at one end of the memory wire and close the jump ring. Make another charm unit and attach it to the loop at the other end of the memory wire. ❖

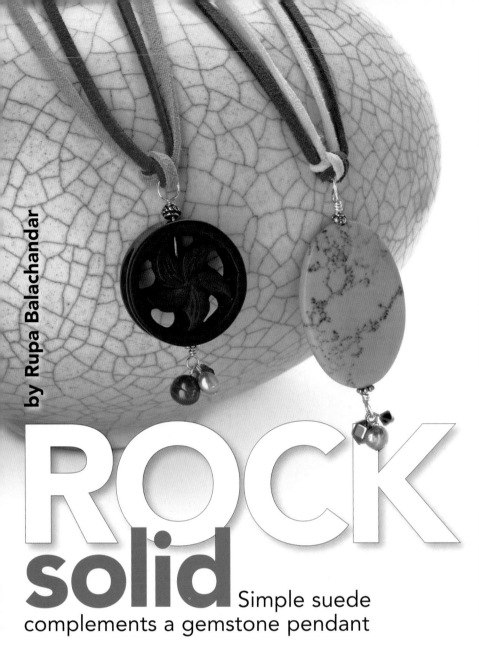

by Rupa Balachandar

ROCK
solid
Simple suede complements a gemstone pendant

For an easy necklace, hang a chunky bail-housed rock from two pieces of suede. Try smooth, faceted, or carved gemstones, such as onyx or dyed green turquoise. Any option will work for casual weekend wear or rockin' till the break of dawn.

Supply List

- 30–40mm pendant, vertically drilled
- **3** 4–8mm accent beads
- **2** 4–6mm flat spacers
- **2** 15–20-in. (38–51cm) pieces 3mm suede cord
- 4 in. (10cm) 20- or 22-gauge half-hard wire
- **3** 1-in. (2.5cm) head pins
- **2** 4mm jump rings
- **2** crimp ends
- lobster claw clasp and soldered jump ring
- chainnose pliers
- roundnose pliers
- diagonal wire cutters
- E6000 adhesive

1 To make a dangle, string an accent bead on a head pin. Make a plain loop (see Basics, p. 12) above the bead. Make a total of three dangles.

2 Cut a 4-in. (10cm) piece of wire. Make a wrapped loop (Basics) at one end. String a flat spacer, the pendant, and a spacer. Above the spacer, make a wrapped loop with the largest part of your roundnose pliers.

Open the loop on each dangle and attach it to the pendant's bottom loop. Close the loops.

3 Determine the finished length of your necklace. (The pink necklace is 15 in./38cm; the green necklace, 16 in./41cm.) Add 1 in. (2.5cm) and cut two pieces of suede cord to that length. Center the pendant's large loop over both pieces. Tie a knot around the loop.

4 Check the fit, allowing 1 in. (2.5cm) for finishing. Trim the cord ends if necessary. Attach a crimp end (Basics) to each pair of cords on each end.

Open a jump ring (Basics). On one end, attach the clasp to the crimp end's loop. Close the jump ring. Repeat on the other end with a soldered jump ring. ✤

Bringing together form and function, this supersized toggle clasp is both a striking centerpiece and an effective closure. Be mindful of proportion when choosing opal nuggets and rondelles, or substitute a less opulent gemstone so the disk remains the central focus.

by Janet Flynn

A bold disk serves two purposes in a toggle-front necklace

Double-

1 Determine the finished length of your necklace. (These are 19 in./48cm.) Add 6 in. (15cm) and cut a piece of beading wire to that length. String: crystal, 4mm spacer, rondelle, 4mm spacer, rondelle, 4mm spacer, rondelle, 4mm spacer, crystal. Center the beads on the wire.

2 On each end, string a 5mm spacer, a nugget, and a 5mm spacer.

EDITOR'S TIP
For a chunkier necklace, string more nuggets and only two rondelles between each crystal.

3 On each end, repeat the patterns in steps 1 and 2 until the necklace is within 1 in. (2.5cm) of the desired length. Check the fit, allowing 2 in. (5cm) for the clasp. Add or remove beads from each end if necessary.

4 On one end, string: two crimp beads, three to five 8º seed beads, first loop of the ring half of the clasp, 8º, second loop of the clasp, three to five 8ºs. Go back through the crimp beads and a few more beads, and crimp the crimp beads (see Basics, p. 12).

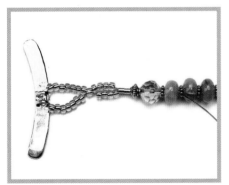

5 On the other end, string: two crimp beads, 12 8ºs, first loop of the bar half of the clasp, 8º, second loop of the clasp, 7 8ºs. Go back through an 8º and string four 8ºs. Go back through the two crimp beads and four more beads. Crimp the crimp beads and trim the excess wire. ✿

Supply List

- 37–56mm toggle clasp (Saki Silver, sakisilver.com)
- **6–8** 12–20mm gemstone nuggets
- **21–27** 10mm rondelles
- **14–18** 9mm round crystals
- 1g 8º seed beads
- **14–18** 5mm flat spacers
- **28–36** 4mm flat spacers
- flexible beading wire, .018 or .019
- **4** crimp beads
- chainnose or crimping pliers
- diagonal wire cutters

duty disk

A glass pendant is the focus of a quick, sparkling necklace and earrings set

by Christianne Camera

Clearly
lovely

Let your style shine through with this glass flower pendant suspended from twinkling crystals and gemstone chips.
It took Mother Nature all winter to create the flowers for her spring garden, but you can make your own delicate bloom – and earrings to match – in under an hour.

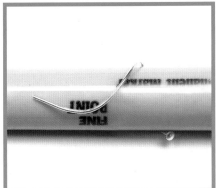

1 **necklace •** On a head pin, string a pendant, two 11º seed beads, a bicone crystal, and an 11º. Make a wrapped loop (see Basics, p. 12) above the top bead.

2 Determine the finished length of your necklace. (These are 17 in./43cm.) Add 6 in. (15cm) and cut a piece of beading wire to that length. On the wire, center: 11º, bicone, 11º, pendant unit, bicone, 11º.

1 **earrings •** Twist a head pin around the barrel of a pen or an object with a similar diameter.

3 On each end, string 1 in. (2.5cm) of gemstone chips, an 11º, a bicone, and an 11º. Repeat until the necklace is within 1 in. of the desired length.

4 On one end, string an 11º, a crimp bead, an 11º, and a lobster claw clasp. Go back through the beads just strung and tighten the wire. Repeat on the other end, substituting a soldered jump ring for the clasp. Check the fit, and add or remove beads from each end if necessary. Flatten the crimp beads (Basics) and trim the excess wire.

2 On the twisted head pin, string: 11º seed bead, bicone crystal, 11º, bicone, 11º, bicone, two 11ºs, bicone, 11º, bicone, 11º, bicone, 11º. Make a plain loop (Basics) above the top bead. With your fingers, form the dangle into a slightly longer, narrower coil.

SupplyList

necklace
- 35mm glass flower pendant (Giralte Gems and Beads, 262-375-5501, giraltegemsandbeads.com)
- 16-in. (41cm) strand 4–6mm gemstone chips
- **12–16** 4mm bicone crystals
- 1g 11º seed beads
- flexible beading wire, .014 or .015
- 3-in. (7.6cm) head pin
- **2** crimp beads
- lobster claw clasp and soldered jump ring
- chainnose pliers
- roundnose pliers
- diagonal wire cutters

earrings
- **12** 4mm bicone crystals
- **16** 11º seed beads
- **2** 1½-in. (3.8cm) head pins
- pair of earring wires
- chainnose pliers
- roundnose pliers
- diagonal wire cutters

EDITOR'S TIP
Use the tip of your chainnose pliers rather than crimping pliers to crimp between two seed beads. It is easier to see the seed beads and, therefore, avoid crushing them.

3 Open the loop of an earring wire and attach the dangle. Close the loop. Make a second earring in the mirror image of the first. ❧

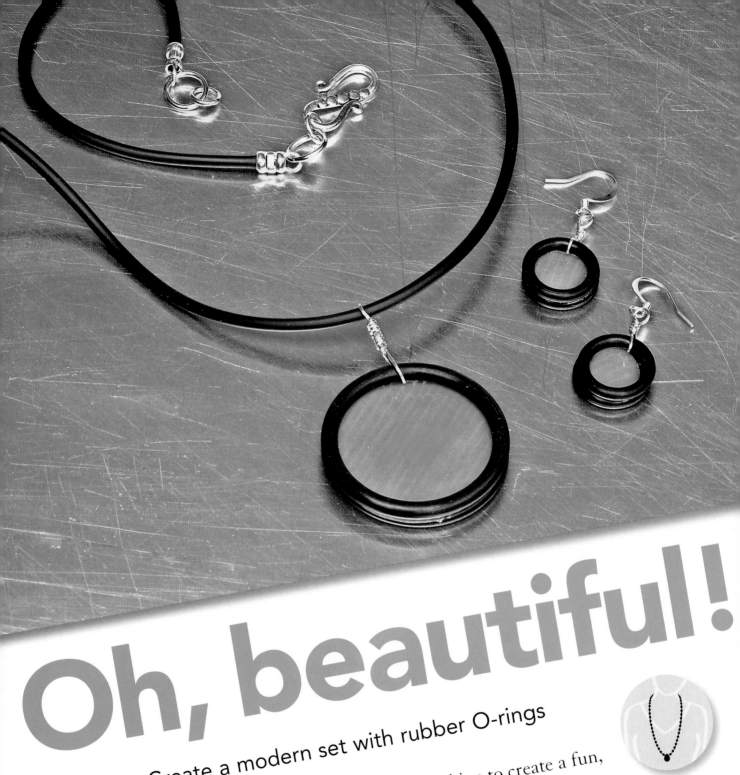

Oh, beautiful!

Create a modern set with rubber O-rings

Window film and rubber O-rings combine to create a fun, unusual necklace. The components might come from the hardware store, but the look says anything but ordinary.

by Cathy Jakicic

1 necklace • String an O-ring on a 6-in. (15cm) piece of wire and make a set of wraps above the O-ring (see Basics, p. 12). With the largest part of your roundnose pliers, make a wrapped loop (Basics) above the wraps, perpendicular to the O-ring.

2 Place the second O-ring on the window film's backing side. Holding the O-ring down gently (so you don't distort the circle), trace the inside of the O-ring with a felt-tip pen. Cut a circle ⅛ in. (3mm) larger than the traced line.

3 Remove the window-film backing and glue the smooth side of the film to the second O-ring.
   Allow the glue to dry, then glue the first O-ring to the ridged side of the film.

4 Determine the finished length of your necklace. (This one is 27 in./69cm.) Subtract 2 in. (5cm) and cut a piece of rubber tubing to that length. Center the O-ring pendant on the tubing. On each end, apply glue to the tubing. Attach a crimp end (Basics) with chainnose pliers.

5 Open a jump ring (Basics) and attach a crimp end and the ring of an S-hook clasp. Close the jump ring. Repeat on the other end, substituting a soldered jump ring for the clasp.

earrings • Follow steps 1–3 of the necklace, using a 15–20mm O-ring and 24-gauge wire. In step 1, make the wrapped loop parallel to the O-ring. Open the loop of an earring wire and attach the dangle. Close the loop. Make a second earring to match the first. ❖

Supply List

necklace
- 3-in. (7.6cm) square of Light Effects window film (lighteffects.com)
- **2** 30–40mm rubber O-rings
- 28 in. (71cm) rubber tubing, 2.5mm diameter
- 6 in. (15cm) 22-gauge square half-hard wire
- **2** 8mm jump rings
- **2** crimp ends
- S-hook clasp and **2** soldered jump rings
- chainnose pliers
- roundnose pliers
- diagonal wire cutters
- G-S Hypo Cement

earrings
- **2** 1-in. (2.5cm) squares of Light Effects window film
- **4** 15–20mm rubber O-rings
- 12 in. (30cm) 24-gauge square half-hard wire
- pair of earring wires
- chainnose pliers
- roundnose pliers
- diagonal wire cutters
- G-S Hypo Cement

EDITOR'S TIP
Browse your local hardware store to find unusual items to use in your projects, like these O-rings and window film.

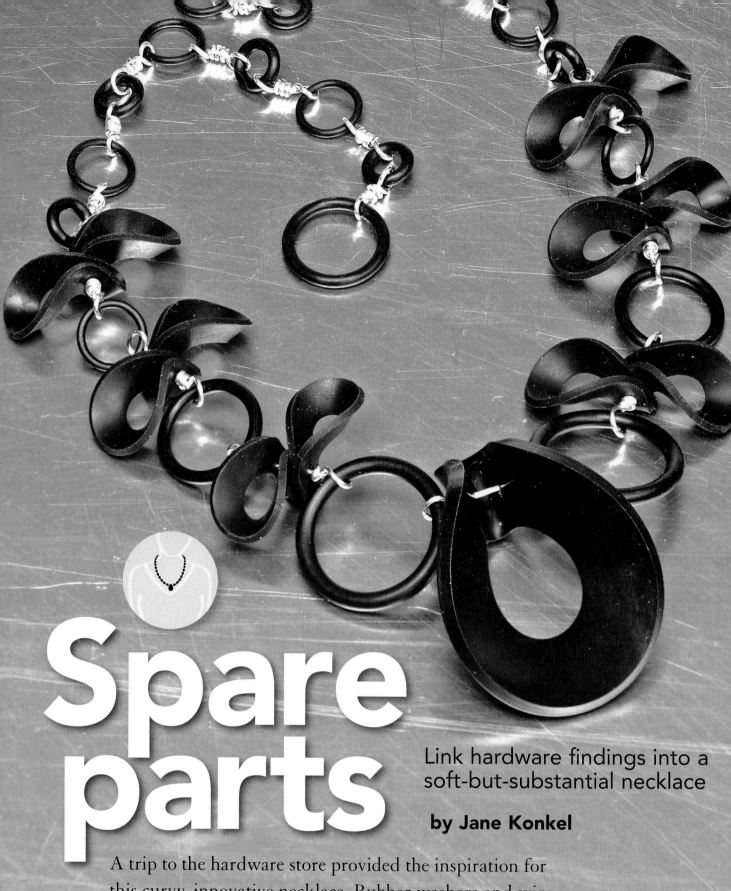

Spare parts

Link hardware findings into a
soft-but-substantial necklace

by Jane Konkel

A trip to the hardware store provided the inspiration for
this curvy, innovative necklace. Rubber washers and wire
come together to create an eye-catching necklace that's
both stylish and practical.

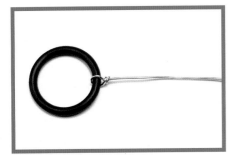

1 Cut a 3-in. (7.6cm) piece of wire. Make the first half of a wrapped loop (see Basics, p. 12) at one end. Attach a #18 O-ring and complete the wraps.

2 Using a tapestry needle, pierce two holes through the top of a 57mm rubber washer, as shown.

3 String the washer on the wire and fold the edges of the washer. Make the first half of a wrapped loop.

Attach a #18 O-ring and complete the wraps.

4 **a** Cut a 3-in. piece of wire. Make the first half of a wrapped loop at one end. Attach the #18 O-ring, and complete the wraps. Repeat on the other side of the necklace.

b Pierce two holes in a 25mm rubber washer as in step 2. Repeat with another 25mm washer. String the first washer on the wire. Turn the second washer upside down and string it on the wire. Make the first half of a wrapped loop. Attach a #13 O-ring to the loop and complete the wraps. Repeat on the other side of the necklace.

5 **a** Cut a 3-in. piece of wire. Make the first half of a wrapped loop at one end. Attach the #13 O-ring and complete the wraps. Repeat on the other side of the necklace.

b Repeat step 4b, substituting a #41 O-ring for the #13 O-ring.

6 **a** Cut a 3-in. piece of wire. Make the first half of a wrapped loop at one end. Attach the #41 O-ring and complete the wraps. Repeat on the other side of the necklace.

b Repeat step 4b, substituting a #78 O-ring for the #13 O-ring.

EDITOR'S TIP
Check the fit as you build the necklace so you don't have to remove any O-rings. This necklace is 18 in. (46cm).

7 Attach an alternating pattern of #41 and #78 O-rings to each side until the necklace is within 1 in. (2.5cm) of the desired length, ending with a #78 O-ring.

Supply List

- 57mm rubber washer
- **12** 25mm rubber washers
- **2** #18 (30mm) rubber O-rings
- **3** #13 (22mm) rubber O-rings
- **8–10** #41 (14mm) rubber O-rings
- **8–10** #78 (11mm) rubber O-rings
- 48–58 in. (1.2–1.5m) 18-gauge half-hard wire
- chainnose pliers
- roundnose pliers
- diagonal wire cutters
- tapestry needle

8 On one end, attach a #13 O-ring. To clasp the necklace, pull the #13 O-ring through the #78 O-ring. ❖

LOSE

Make fashion-forward bracelets with surplus beads

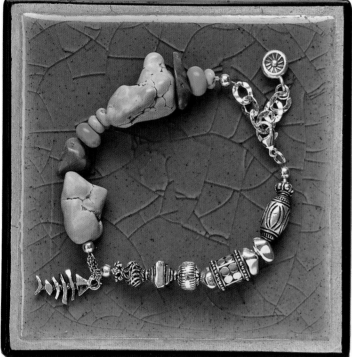

YOUR

by Carol McKinney

RESERVE

Chances are, you already have the necessary provisions for several of these stylish bracelets. Unearth your accumulated odds and ends, gemstone nuggets, forgotten trinkets, and unique pieces left over from previous projects. Throw caution to the wind as you create your own distinctive designs.

1 gemstone-chip bracelet • Cut a 2-in. (5cm) piece of wire. Make a plain loop (see Basics, p. 12) on one end. String a bead and make the first half of a wrapped loop (Basics) above the bead. Make 8–10 bead units.

2 Attach one bead unit to the loop of a lobster claw clasp and complete the wraps.

3 Cut a 1-in. (2.5cm) piece of chain. Attach each of the remaining bead units to the chain, and complete the wraps.

Open a jump ring (Basics) and attach a charm to the chain. Repeat with the remaining charms.

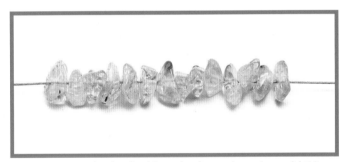

4 Determine the finished length of your bracelet, add 5 in. (13cm), and cut a piece of beading wire to that length. String approximately 2 in. of gemstone chips.

5 String approximately 4½ in. (11.4cm) of beads and spacers.

6 On one end, string a crimp bead, a spacer, and the lobster claw clasp from step 2. Go back through the beads just strung and tighten the wire. Repeat on the other end, substituting a split ring for the clasp. Check the fit, and add or remove beads from each end if necessary. Crimp the crimp beads (Basics) and trim the excess wire.

7 Attach the chain dangle to the split ring.

1 silver bracelet • Determine the finished length of your bracelet, add 5 in. (13cm), and cut a piece of beading wire to that length. Cut the beading wire in half. On one wire, string approximately 3 in. (7.6cm) of silver beads and spacers. On the other wire, string 3 in. of beads and nuggets.

2 On one end of each strand, string a crimp bead and a 4mm spacer, then go through the same soldered jump ring. Go back through the beads just strung and tighten the wires. Crimp the crimp beads.

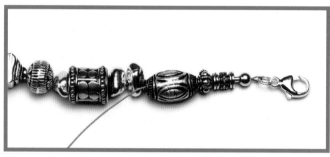

3 Attach a lobster claw clasp to a split ring. On one end, string a crimp bead, a 4mm spacer, and the split ring. Go back through the beads just strung and tighten the wire.

4 Repeat step 3 on the other end, substituting a 1-in. (2.5cm) piece of chain for the split ring and clasp. Check the fit, and add or remove beads if necessary. Crimp the crimp beads and trim the excess wire.

5 Using a split ring, attach a charm to the center jump ring. ✤

EDITOR'S TIP

For the silver bracelet, attach a charm to the last chain link with a jump ring. Not only is the charm decorative, but it also helps to locate and steady the end of the chain when clasping the lobster claw clasp.

SupplyList

gemstone-chip bracelet
- **20–30** 4–26mm beads, spacers, and charms
- **12–32** 4–6mm gemstone chips
- **2** 4mm round spacers
- flexible beading wire, .014 or .015
- 16–20 in. (41–51cm) 22-gauge half-hard wire
- 1 in. (2.5cm) chain, 5mm links
- 4mm jump ring for each charm
- **2** crimp beads
- lobster claw clasp and 6mm split ring
- chainnose pliers
- roundnose pliers
- diagonal wire cutters
- crimping and split-ring pliers (optional)

silver bracelet
- **12–16** 4–20mm silver beads, spacers, and charms
- **6–10** 6–25mm gemstone beads and nuggets
- **4** 4mm round spacers
- flexible beading wire, .014 or .015
- 1 in. (2.5cm) chain, 5mm links
- 6mm soldered jump ring
- 6mm split ring
- **4** crimp beads
- lobster claw clasp and 6mm split ring
- chainnose or crimping pliers
- diagonal wire cutters
- split-ring pliers (optional)

Contributors

Betsy Baker has an international background that is reflected in her work. Contact Betsy through her Web site, stonehouse-studio.com.

Rupa Balachandar specializes in sterling silver pendants that incorporate unusual gemstones. Visit her Web site, rupab.com.

Denise Baum can be reached at wristcraft@hotmail.com.

Paulette Biedenbender owns the retail store Bead Needs in Hales Corners, Wis. Reach her at (414) 529-5211, or visit her Web site at beadneedsllc.com.

Contact **Teri Bienvenue** in care of *BeadStyle*.

Christianne and Maria Camera co-own Bella Bella! in Milwaukee. Contact them in care of *BeadStyle*.

Todd Canyon Sinclair is a jewelry designer based in New York. Contact Todd at canyonsinclair@earthlink.net.

Contact **Katee Lee Chimpouras** at chimps@cac.net.

Nina Cooper owns Nina Designs, serving bead enthusiasts worldwide with creative findings and jewelry designs. Visit ninadesigns.com.

Amy DeLeo and Lindsay O. Vance sell their one-of-a-kind handcrafted jewelry through their Web site, jujubead.com.

Contact **Miachelle DePiano** through her Web site, cosmopolitanaccessories.net.

Yailis Feliciano finds inspiration in the beauty of her native Puerto Rico. She offers private jewelry-making lessons in her home in Westchester County, N.Y. Visit myspecialdesign.com.

After **Janet Flynn** discovered beads in 1990, her life was never the same. Janet teaches beading nationwide. Contact her through her Web site, janetflynn.com.

Naomi Fujimoto is Senior Editor of *BeadStyle*.

Shruti Gautam Dev creates lampworked beads and incorporates them into her creations. Contact her at shrutigdev@gmail.com or visit artyzenworld.blogspot.com.

Sue Godfrey's designs are available at several art jewelry boutiques. She works and teaches classes at Midwest Beads in Brookfield, Wis. Contact Sue at highstrungsue@wi.rr.com.

Karen Gollhardt is a jewelry designer and glass artist. Contact her through her Web site, karilyndesigns.com.

Diana Grossman is based in New York. Visit her Web site, deenmiele.com.

Lindsay Haedt is Editorial Associate of *BeadStyle*.

Catherine Hodge designs jewelry with a focus on beauty and balance. Contact her through her Web site, catherinemarissa.com

Contact **Jill Italiano** through her Web site, jillidesigns.com.

Cathy Jakicic is Editor of *BeadStyle*.

Steven James incorporates beads and jewelry making into home décor. Visit Steven's Web site, macaroniandglitter.com.

See more of **Linda Jones'** work on her Web site, wirejewellery.co.uk.

Contact **Eva Kapitany** in care of *BeadStyle*.

Jane Konkel is Associate Editor of *BeadStyle*.

Contact **Nancy Kugel** in care of *BeadStyle*.

Contact **Carol McKinney** through her Web site, carolsjewelryandgifts.com.

Karen Meyer creates lampworked beads and jewelry featuring her glass beads. Visit her Web site, karenbeads.com.

Irina Miech owns Eclectica in Brookfield, Wis. She is the author of *Metal Clay for Beaders* and many articles on beading and jewelry design projects. Contact Irina through her Web site, eclecticabeads.com.

Stacey Neilson has been beading since the early 1970s, and now shares her knowledge by teaching. Contact Stacey through her Web site, www.yellowbrickroad.ie.

Rachel Nelson-Smith sells kits for the Krystallos ladder cuff. Contact Rachel through her Web site, msrachel.com.

Anne Nikolai Kloss is a highly regarded bead artist and instructor from Waukesha, Wis. Contact Anne at annekloss@mac.com.

Contact **Lea Rose Nowicki** in care of *BeadStyle*.

Contact **Kathie Pemberton** through her Web site, tulipjewellery.co.uk.

Judy Pifko handcrafts original jewelry using gemstones, pearls, crystals, and sterling silver. Contact Judy at pifko@shaw.ca.

Contact **Tyrenia Pyskacek** in care of *BeadStyle*.

Shannon Reeves works at Knot Just Beads in Mobile, Ala., where she designs and sells her jewelry. Contact Shannon at thereeves@aol.com.

Ronna Sarvas Weltman uses silver, semi-precious stones, metal clay, vintage trade beads, and found objects to craft one-of-a-kind artisan beads and jewelry. See more of her work on her Web site, ronnaround.com.

Florence Sauerbrey, originally from France, now lives in Cape Cod. A painter and a writer, she loves to play with colors. Contact Florence at f.sauerbrey@verizon.net.

Brenda Schweder offers kits through her Web site, brendaschweder.com. Brenda is a frequent *BeadStyle* contributor and coauthor of the magazine's Fashion Forecast column.

Contact **Jennifer Seneca** through her Web site, bluefrogjewelry.com.

Sara Strauss was trained in jewelry design at the Fashion Institute of Technology in New York. See more of her work at sgsjewelry.com.

Contact **Stacie Thompson** in care of *BeadStyle*.

Contact **Susan Tobias** in care of *BeadStyle*.

Contact **Helene Tsigistras** at htsigistras@kalmbach.com.

Contact **Karen Woodson** in care of her Web site, toocutebeads.com.

Jean Yates is based in Westchester County, N.Y. Her specialty is wirework, integrating polymer and lampworked beads into her designs. Contact Jean through her Web site, prettykittydogmoonjewelry.com.